HISTORY & CRITICISM

HISTORY &
CRITICISM

Dominick LaCapra

CORNELL UNIVERSITY PRESS

ITHACA AND LONDON

First published 1985 by Cornell University Press.
First printing, Cornell Paperbacks, 1987.
Second printing, Cornell Paperbacks, 1989.

International Standard Book Number 0-8014-1788-0 (cloth)
International Standard Book Number 0-8014-9324-2 (paper)
Library of Congress Catalog Card Number 84-16990

Printed in the United States of America

*Librarians: Library of Congress cataloging information
appears on the last page of the book.*

*The paper in this book is acid-free and meets
the guidelines for permanence and durability of
the Committee on Production Guidelines for Book Longevity
of the Council on Library Resources.*

When a man has his mouth so full of food that he is prevented from eating, and is like to starve in consequence, does giving him food consist in stuffing still more of it in his mouth, or does it consist in taking some of it away, so that he can begin to eat? And so also when a man has much knowledge, and his knowledge has little or no significance for him, does a rational communication consist in giving him more knowledge, even supposing that he is loud in his insistence that this is what he needs, or does it not rather consist in taking some of it away? When an author communicates a portion of the knowledge that such a well-informed man has, in a form which makes it seem strange to him, it is as if he took his knowledge away from him, at least provisionally, until by having overcome the opposition of the form he succeeds in assimilating it. . . .

The comical is always the mark of maturity; but it is important that the new shoot should be ready to appear under this maturity, and that the *vis comica* should not stifle the pathetic, but rather serve as an indication that a new pathos is beginning.

SØREN KIERKEGAARD,
Concluding Unscientific Postscript

Contents

Preface

THIS book does not argue one dominant thesis, but it is activated by a number of related concerns: the complex nature of history as a "dialogical" exchange both with the past and with others inquiring into it; the role of critical theory in historical understanding; the relation of historiography to other disciplines; and the need for historians to respond creatively to newer challenges in contemporary thought. From a long-term perspective on problems, I try to revive a Renaissance ideal of historiography that is largely out of favor at present—one in which scholarly research is intimately linked to "rhetorical" and ethicopolitical discourse. In more contemporary terms, I am especially interested in the relations between intellectual history, which must develop modes of critical and self-critical interpretation, and social history, which has been preoccupied with the attempt to elaborate methods to investigate the contexts of interpretation. I continue to believe that historians have much to learn from disciplines such as literary criticism and philosophy where debates over the nature of interpretation have been particularly lively in the recent past. I would like to help bring historiography to the point at which it is able to enter those debates in a more even-handed way—not simply as a repository of facts or a neopositivistic stepchild of social science, and certainly not as a mythologized locus for some prediscursive image of "reality," but as a critical voice in the disciplines addressing problems of understanding and explanation.

Given pronounced tendencies in other subdisciplines of historiography at the present time, it may be little more than an anachronism that intellectual history still finds itself in departments of history. It might more plausibly be situated, along with comparative literature and Continental philosophy, in something like a department of comparative studies or a humanities center. In institutional terms, the problem is a familiar one: divorce or the transformation of a questionable situation. I would like to believe that this option is overdrawn, although there may be good reasons for overcoming institutional inertia and shifting the lines between certain existing disciplines. I would also like to believe that the bonds holding intellectual historians to departments of history are not limited to personal ties to colleagues and the comforts of the silken cords of tradition. In any event, the intellectual task is to turn what may be anachronistic into a source of new possibilities in historiography itself—to make the trope linking history and criticism an acceptable oxymoron. For a very long time, intellectual historians have tried to adapt to procedures in other sectors of historiography, and, for a briefer time, they have defensively looked to social history for guidance. The very idea of a "total history" has often been little more than a blind behind which social history could be transformed into the mother hen of historiography in general. As the following essays will show, I do think that there is much room for interaction between intellectual history and social history. But for that interaction to be viable, it must take place between perspectives that are relatively well matched in strength and urgency—perspectives that can pose stimulating challenges to one another. Beyond these disciplinary matters, however, the following essays also hint at a more difficult question: how can history be not simply a profession but a vocation?

No one could deny the gains that advanced professionalization and specialization have brought to historiography. But in so far as the study of history is a vocation as well as a profession, historical research cannot be completely confined within disciplinary boundaries or subjected to evaluation by professional tribunals alone. It is accountable to a larger, often divided audience. And it may journey into areas normally seen as the prerogatives of other disciplines. By the very nature of its "objects" of study, intellectual history necessarily migrates across disciplinary and departmental lines. Its liminal, indeed joker-like, status becomes especially pronounced as intellectual historians recognize themselves as both intellectuals and historians. But, as these essays indicate, I would also argue that all forms of historiography might benefit from modes of critical reading premised on the conviction that documents are texts that supplement or rework "reality" and not mere sources that divulge facts about "reality." In this respect, there is a need for *Quellenkritik* (the critique of sources) in a new and at times unfamiliar sense. To the extent that critical reading and self-critical reflection are requisites of a cognitively responsible historiography, there is a sense in which all history must indeed be intellectual history. All history, moreover, must more or less blindly encounter the problem of a transferential relation to the past whereby the processes at work in the object of study acquire their displaced analogues in the historian's account. Coming to terms with transference in an exchange with the past may be the issue that confronts historiography with its most engaging and unsettling challenge.

The chapters of this book were originally written as lectures. I have decided not to eliminate the signs of oral delivery that some of them (particularly chapters 4 and 5) still bear because I believe that they render more accessible the arguments I am trying to make. The book as a whole is intended as an attempt to articulate certain ideas in a relatively "popularized"—but I hope not vulgarized—

form. I especially try to address issues in ways that connect with problems that historians and their readership will recognize as relevant to historical research. (The fourth chapter, however, may at times call upon background knowledge that is more prevalent among literary critics.) More generally, I attempt to broach a number of difficult questions in a manner that may be of interest to "experts" while remaining intelligible to a general reader. In the process, I make use of relatively "theoretical" discourse in order to further both a certain self-understanding and a significantly modified practice of historiography. I would not deny that history is in important respects a craft or, indeed, an art that is learned and plied on the basis of tacit knowledge and subtle know-how. But I would resist the complacent if not reactionary version of this idea that enjoins the historian to "imbibe" the wisdom of eminent practitioners and bask in the light of sun-drenched exemplars. Historiography that turns away from critical reflection and ideological issues is not a craft. It is little more than a pampered profession.

"Is Everyone a *Mentalité* Case? Transference and the 'Culture' Concept" appeared in *History and Theory* 23 (1984), no. 3, © 1984 by Wesleyan University and is reprinted by permission. The other essays are published here for the first time.

DOMINICK LACAPRA

Ithaca, New York

HISTORY & CRITICISM

1

Rhetoric and History

On the coming of evening, I return to my house and enter
my study; and at the door I take off my every-day clothes,
covered with mud and dust, and I put on garments regal
and courtly; and, thus reclothed appropriately, I enter the
ancient courts of ancient men, where, being lovingly
received by them, I feed on that food that alone is mine
and for which I was born, where I am not ashamed to
speak with them and to ask them the reason of their
actions; and they, out of their humanity, answer me; and
for four hours of time I feel no boredom, I forget every
trouble, I do not fear poverty, death does not terrify me; I
am completely transferred into them.

NICCOLÒ MACHIAVELLI

THE study of rhetoric is once again on the agenda of humanistic
studies. Scholars in various disciplines have become sensitive
to the losses involved in its eclipse over the last three centuries, and
a flurry of interest has marked the recent past. Historians themselves have renewed inquiry into the role of rhetoric in their objects
of study.[1] But their research has often tended to lack the reflexive
and self-critical component that is more evident in certain sectors
of literary criticism and philosophy. Understandably fearful of the
involuted, narcissistic extremes of self-reflection, historians have

1. See, for example, Bernard Bailyn, *The Ideological Origins of the American
Revolution* (Cambridge, Mass., 1967).

paid scant attention to their own rhetoric and to the role of the
rhetorical (including the rhetoric of so-called "hard" science) in
constituting their discipline.

But if historians are tempted to look for guidance in literary
criticism and philosophy, they are confronted by a number of
obstacles. Rhetoric has often been in the scapegoated position of
the radically "other"—sometimes elevated as the marginal hope of
language or more frequently debased as its common whore. It is
usually contrasted with logic or science, which may assume the
figurative position of legitimate "wife" of the mind. The tendency
to expect everything or nothing at all from rhetoric is still prevalent, as is the ambivalence the term itself seems to engender.

No doubt the quest for an inclusive and exhaustive definition of
rhetoric is an impossible one. But some working definition is
inevitable, and it will operate in any event. Recent theorists have
tried to renew the understanding of rhetoric both by historical
inquiry into its vicissitudes over time and by exploring the gap
between the exalted and low-life statuses attributed to it. Yet
diversity of approach and fluidity of comprehension have often
characterized recent reinterpretations.

It is provisionally useful to distinguish among three significant
orientations that may be combined in various ways in the works of
different scholars: (1) The revision of older conceptions of rhetoric
in the light of modern linguistics and discourse analysis. This
tendency may go so far as to induce an identification of rhetoric
with vast segments of discourse, conceivably all of it with the
possible exception of highly formalized metalanguages.[2] Less ex-

2. Paolo Valesio asserts: "Rhetoric is the functional organization of discourse,
within its social and cultural context, in all its aspects, exception made for its
realization as a strictly formal metalanguage—in formal logic, mathematics, and
in the sciences whose metalanguages share the same features. In other words:
rhetoric is *all* of language, in its realization as discourse. For, to exclude strictly
formalized metalanguages from the domain of rhetoric (and even this tentatively—
until one investigates the possible rhetorical elements in those metalanguages) is to
discard something that is not, properly speaking, language; the catholicity of
rhetoric, that ranges over the whole of linguistic structure, is thus confirmed rather
than weakened." *Novantiqua: Rhetorics as Contemporary Theory* (Bloomington,
Ind., 1980), p. 7.

pansive but nonetheless ambitious attempts to reconsider the scope of rhetoric may address the issues of argument and style, the nature of deliberative, forensic, and epideictic oratory, or the relations among *inventio* (ideas and arguments), *dispositio* (composition), and *elocutio* (choice and arrangement of words).[3] (2) The elaboration of a theory of figures, tropes, and "literary" or "poetic" uses of language.[4] Here the scope of rhetoric is narrowed, but analyses of it may become more finely tuned or even hermetically technical in nature. This second tendency may nonetheless lead back to the first when tropes are accorded an originary or generative function in language and seen as giving rise to other uses (such as argument, emplotment, and ideology).[5] (3) A focus on problems of persuasion and audience that may convert Aristotle's definition of rhetoric into a program for an aesthetics of reception.[6]

The most challenging feature shared by these tendencies is the idea that rhetoric is a dimension of all language use rather than a separable set of uses or a realm of discourse. The question then becomes how rhetoric does and should interact with other dimensions of discourse in various disciplines. Historians have shown relatively little interest in this problem, in good part because they continue to confide in a "documentary" or "objectivist" model of knowledge that is typically blind to its own rhetoric. Indeed this

3. See, for example, Gérard Genette, *Figures I* (Paris, 1966), *Figures II* (Paris, 1969), and *Figures III* (Paris, 1972); Ch. Perelman and L. Olbrechts-Tyteca, *Traité de l'argumentation: la Nouvelle Rhétorique* (Paris, 1958); and Paul Ricoeur, *The Rule of Metaphor* (Toronto, 1977).

4. See, for example, J. Dubois et al., *Rhétorique générale* (Paris, 1970), and Paul de Man, *Allegories of Reading* (New Haven, 1979). De Man asserts: "The grammatical model of the question becomes rhetorical not when we have, on the one hand, a literal meaning and on the other hand a figural meaning, but when it is impossible to decide by grammatical or other linguistic devices which of the two meanings (that can be entirely incompatible) prevails. . . . Although it would perhaps be somewhat remote from common usage, I would not hesitate to equate the rhetorical, figural potentiality of language with literature itself" (p. 10).

5. See Hayden V. White, *Metahistory* (Baltimore, 1973) and *Tropics of Discourse* (Baltimore, 1978).

6. Here I would simply mention the different approaches to this problem taken by Wayne Booth, Hans Robert Jauss, Wolfgang Iser, and Stanley Fish.

model has been effective in placating or neutralizing concerns that motivate the work of the new rhetoricians.

What is a "documentary" model of knowledge and how prevalent has it been in the self-understanding of historians or, in more problematic form, in their actual practice in writing history? In addressing these questions in a short space, I can only offer answers that threaten to be caricatures, and I shall hazard generalizations that would require qualification and refinement in any longer treatment.

In a documentary model, the basis of research is "hard" fact derived from the critical sifting of sources, and the purpose of historiography is either to furnish narrative accounts and "thick descriptions" of documented facts or to submit the historical record to analytic procedures of hypothesis-formation, testing, and explanation. The historical imagination is limited to plausibly filling gaps in the record, and "throwing new light" on a phenomenon requires the discovery of hitherto unknown information. It does not mean seeing the phenomenon differently or transforming our understanding of it through reinterpretation. Indeed all sources tend to be treated in narrowly documentary terms, that is, in terms of factual or referential propositions that may be derived from them to provide information about specific times and places. There is, moreover, an explicit or implicit hierarchy among sources whereby a preferential position is accorded to seemingly direct informational documents such as bureaucratic reports, wills, registers, diaries, eye-witness accounts, and so forth. If other texts are treated at all, they are reduced to elements that are either redundant or merely supplementary (and, if not checked against "hard" data, purely suggestive) with respect to privileged "informational" documents. The narrowly documentary use of sources helps to account for the marginalization of intellectual history in the discipline and for its adaptation to a conception of research that ill suits it, since its "artifacts" pose the most blatant resistance to narrowly documentary readings.

In the recent past, much attention has been paid to mechanisms of diffusion and the documentation of how texts and other artifacts are circulated and used in society, but little notice has been granted to the precise process whereby complex texts undergo transformation into specific use and exchange values—a process whose investigation would confront the historian with problems not reducible to a truncated documentary framework. Indeed, it is at times assumed that the only significant historical questions are those that can be answered by empirical (preferably archival) research. Interpretation requiring a less restricted interchange between the historian and the object of study is confined at best to an ancillary status, and a rather unproblematic notion of "context" becomes the key explanatory variable (if not the equivalent of historical "reality"). The notion of context may even serve as a way to get around texts and the problem of interpreting or reading them other than in reductively documentary ways. A wedge is driven between history and critical theory, and while the latter may suggest hypotheses or enable the historian, in a brief conclusion, to change "voices" and pronounce a few sententious *obiter dicta,* any sustained interaction between history and critical theory is condemned as "unhistorical." Reconstruction of the past, putatively "in its own terms," remains the overriding consideration, and the objective is to be as objective as possible by controlling for "bias" or "subjective preference" in researching problems and testing hypotheses. The affirmation of an objectivist frame of reference may be fostered by anxiety over a "relapse" into "relativism," and the charge of "projection" may be directed at the historian whose interpretation—or entire interpretative orientation—one rejects. Rarely raised is the question of whether this entire way of framing issues rests on dubious assumptions and needs to be rethought.

The difficulty is that a restricted documentary or objectivist model takes what is in certain respects a necessary condition or a crucial dimension of historiography and converts it into a virtually exhaustive definition. It also diverts attention from the way "documents" are themselves texts that "process" or rework "reality" and require a critical reading that goes beyond traditional philological forms of *Quellenkritik*. It thereby obscures certain aspects both of the past and of the historian's discourse about it.

In a recent article, H. Stuart Hughes went so far as to see a "regression" in contemporary historiography to a "primitive positivism," and he made this provocative observation: "Historians in this country seem to have forgotten—if they ever properly learned—the simple truth that what one may call progress in their endeavors comes not merely through the discovery of new materials but at least as much through a *new reading* of materials already available."[7] After noting the recent spate of methodological studies in professional historiography, Laurence Veysey—an historian the direction of whose research is significantly different from that of Hughes's—nonetheless commented with a mild touch of irony and a large dose of hyperbole: "With all this greater sophistication about historical argument, it remains true that the very highest amount of prestige is still awarded to an historian who uncovers (no matter how he does it) some incontestable but previously unknown fact of undeniably major importance."[8] While one may object that the greatest prestige often goes to the historian who revises standard accounts on the basis of massive archival research, one may nonetheless suggest that Mr. Gradgrind has been the modern historian's alter ego. And there is a sense in which the shock of recognition, however addled with mixed feelings, that is evoked by Dickens's caricature (or, more subtly, by the portrait of Mr. Casaubon in George Eliot's *Middlemarch*) must be part of the professional historian's fate. Indeed, to the extent that components of a documentary model constitute a necessary condition of professional historiography, the historian will face the recurrent temptations of making a fetish of archival

7. "Contemporary Historiography: Progress, Paradigms, and the Regression toward Positivism," in *Progress and Its Discontents,* ed. Gabriel A. Almond, Marvin Chodorow, and Roy Harvey Harris (Berkeley, Los Angeles, and London, 1982), p. 245.

8. "The United States," in the *International Handbook of Historical Studies: Contemporary Research and Theory,* ed. Georg G. Iggers and Harold T. Parker (Westport, Conn., 1979), p. 168.

research, attempting to discover some "unjustly neglected" fact, figure, or phenomenon, and dreaming of a "thesis" to which his or her proper name may be attached (or a Heath pamphlet devoted). But a more interactive model of discourse that allows for the mutual—at times the mutually challenging—interchange of "documentary" and "rhetorical" dimensions of language may further a broader conception of historical knowledge itself—one that gives a new twist to the venerable idea that history is both "science" and "art."

How to confront the limitations of a documentary model without simply converting all history into metahistory or denying the role of referential uses of language in the past and in the historian's account of it is a complicated issue, but one the historian is increasingly forced to face. What should be obvious is that "objectivism" and "relativism" (or "subjectivism") are false options forming part of a larger complex that has to be situated and overcome. The problem in this respect is how to relate, in theory and discursive practice, the historian's use of texts as documents in the inferential reconstruction of "reality" (or the "broader context") and his or her critical reading of texts (including items usually referred to as documents) in a manner that may itself affect both the conception of former "reality" and activity in the present. There are signs that historians are becoming aware of this problem, but the articulation of it in a cogent form is still elusive despite important initiatives in the recent past.[9]

To give some idea of the prevalence of a documentary model, I would like to discuss briefly a few books: *History* by John Higham with Felix Gilbert and Leonard Krieger (1965);[10] *Historical Studies Today* edited by Felix Gilbert and Stephen Graubard (1972);[11] and *The Past Before Us* edited by Michael Kammen (1980).[12]

9. In addition to the previously cited works of Hayden White, see those of Michel de Certeau, especially *L'écriture de l'histoire* (Paris, 1975) and *L'invention du quotidien* (Paris, 1980).

10. Englewood Cliffs, 1965.

11. New York, 1972.

12. Ithaca, N.Y., 1980.

These books are of special interest because they span the last
generation and include "state-of-the-art" appraisals written by
notable historians who were more or less explicitly charged to
represent the "official consciousness" of the discipline in general
and/or their subdiscipline in particular. Given the more idiosyn-
cratic initiatives and the inevitable differences in quality that nonetheless appear in the contributions, it would be excessive to claim a
"paradigmatic" status for these texts. And, in view of the limitations of this essay, I shall be highly selective in discussing them,
thus not furnishing a content analysis—much less a "textual"
reading—of them. But I think my use of these texts, while itself
threatening to become too "documentary," may still have some
indicative value concerning the state of the discipline. I shall also
refer to a book from which I have already quoted and which has
generally received less attention than these three: the *International
Handbook of Historical Studies, Contemporary Research and
Theory* edited by Georg G. Iggers and Harold T. Parker (1979). It
too tries to survey the field, often calling upon younger scholars as
contributors. What is especially striking, I think, is that contributors to all these volumes tend to accept as unquestioned assumptions the basic constituents of what I have delineated as a documentary model of historical understanding, and at times they take
it in more pronounced, indeed extreme directions than ones I have
mentioned thus far. Most often this model is qualified or ironized
(if at all) only in the most tentative fashion. The very fact that this
model functions largely as a tacit assumption attests to its deep-
rooted nature and to its force. At present it may be an essential
prerequisite of mutual recognition among historians. Moreover, if
there is some "evolution" over time in these books, it would seem
to be in the direction of an increasingly secure, "professionalized"
conception of historiography.

The volume by Higham, Gilbert, and Krieger is initially surpris-
ing in that it contains little on the specific problems of intellectual
history in spite of the fact that the three authors are well known in
the discipline as practitioners of that subdiscipline. This feature of

the volume is a sign of the degree of integration of intellectual history with history in general for the authors, as well as of the role of uniform assumptions in their approach to both the subdiscipline and the larger discipline. Yet the authors display a sustained interest in theoretical issues and a modulated defense of a documentary ideal. They evince little sense of crisis about the state of the profession but instead project an air of confidence tempered by concern about the danger of over-specialization.

Higham offers an especially impressive survey of the history of historiography in the United States covering the age of "scientific" history at the turn of the century, the reaction to it on the part of reformist, present-minded "New Historians" (James Harvey Robinson, Carl Becker, and Charles Beard), and the recent attempt at a more synthetic understanding of historical research. Higham's analysis of the past is enlivened by sharp criticism of certain tendencies, but his treatment of the contemporary state of the discipline is optimistic and somewhat lacking in the critical edge of his retrospect. The historiography of his own time has, he feels, combined the best of older scientific history and the more recent New History while avoiding sterile debates and the "rarefied regions of the philosophy of history."[13] The focus on practical methodology has enabled historians to satisfy the professional demands of their peers while also addressing the needs of a popular audience. Higham asserts: "Although its critical operations are exacting, its fundamental tasks of organizing data into a design and thereby recreating the life of the past does not depend on any systematic methodology. Nor has history a special language of its own. Consequently, professional historians are unable to immure themselves completely within a specialized sphere, and writers unblessed with special training are often capable of doing important historical work."[14]

13. *History,* p. 89.
14. Ibid., pp. 68–69. Contrast the comments of Hayden White: "Since the second half of the nineteenth century, history has become increasingly the refuge of all those 'sane' men who excel at finding the simple in the complex and the familiar

One may wonder whether the historian's attempt to mediate between difficult texts or expert knowledge and popular understanding might generate more tension than Higham allows. And does the desire to find order in chaos or a design in the carpet of the past obscure the interaction between order and challenges to it both in the object of study and in the historian's discourse about it? The postulates of order and ordinary understanding are two of the most important aspects of a certain model of knowledge. They are seconded in the informative and urbane analyses of Krieger and Gilbert, who extend the investigation to European history. Krieger stresses the way historiography seeks unity and knowledge that renders the unfamiliar familiar in the reader's mind. "Ultimately, then, the two faces of European history in America that make up its contemporary status—its position in America and its position in the world—are one. It has helped to build into the structure of knowledge meanings that are general without being abstract, and it has contributed its bit thereby to the preparation of men's minds for the admission of the hitherto unknown in ways that refine but do not violate their fundamental ideas. And this, after all, is the prime function of the historical sense."[15]

Felix Gilbert takes Krieger's identification of the historical sense and common sense a little further in a statement that both concludes his own contribution and is quoted in the preface by the general editor of the Ford Humanities Project of which this volume was one installment. Thus Gilbert's words provide an inaugural and a terminal frame for the book as a whole:

> The foremost task of the historian is to regain an image of the past in which history emerges as the conceptualization of a

---

in the strange. . . . What is usually called the 'training' of the historian consists for the most part of study in a few languages, journeyman work in the archives, and the performance of a few set exercises to acquaint him with standard reference works and journals in his field. For the rest, a general experience of human affairs, reading in peripheral fields, self-discipline, and *Sitzfleisch* are all that are necessary." "The Burden of History," in *Tropics of Discourse*, pp. 30 and 40. This essay was first published in 1966.

15. *History*, p. 313.

unified process. For the existence of history as a profession and as an independent field depends on the conception of the past as a totality. But the need for reconstructing a historical consciousness that integrates the present with the past is much more than the professional interest of the historian. It is rooted in the general need of our time. Because history is the study of man in his social conditions, the establishment of the relation of the past to the present reasserts the role of man in a world that appears to slide out of human control. And justification for the concern with history is the conviction that "there is no future without a past and there is no past without a future."[16]

The dream of a "total history" corroborating the historian's own desire for mastery of a documentary repertoire and furnishing the reader with a vicarious sense of—or perhaps a project for—control in a world out of joint has of course been a lodestar of historiography from Hegel to the *Annales* school. And its intellectual and practical limitations are only recently becoming evident in the historical profession.[17] On a more pragmatic level, Higham, as I have intimated, believed that historians of his own time were on the verge of attaining a synthetic balance in their approach to the problems that had beleaguered their predecessors:

On the score of relativism, historians did not swing back to the simple faith in a hard, external reality, and the accompanying distrust of their own shaping imagination, that characterized scientific history. The age of realism and naturalism in American culture had passed. Historians no longer considered their own subjectivity as exclusively a problem or a barrier to struggle against. It was that, of course. The task of historiography would always require the utmost divestment of bias and the penetration of a realm beyond the immediate self and its immediate society. But historians now knew that this achieve-

16. Ibid., p. 387.
17. See, for example, Roger Chartier, "Intellectual History or Sociocultural History? The French Trajectories," and Dominick LaCapra, "Rethinking Intellectual History and Reading Texts," in *Modern European Intellectual History: Reappraisals and New Perspectives* (Ithaca, N.Y., 1982), ed. Dominick LaCapra and Steven L. Kaplan.

ment is not simply an act of self-effacement, not an effort to register passively the harmonies of an evolutionary pattern. It calls for a creative outreach of imagination and draws upon all the resources of the historian's human condition.[18]

Higham's belief in the passing of realistic faith may have been premature.[19] In any event, his admirably balanced affirmation nonetheless leaves one asking what are the valid uses of language in historiography that escape the polarities of self-effacing objectivity and subjective bias. And does the "creative outreach" of the historian's imagination involve an exchange with the past not limited to a sympathetic identification with the experience of people in other times and places?

Higham stresses the conciliatory nature of liberal, civilized debate among historians as well as the effort to unite the contribution of social science with an artistic idea of the historian's craft.

18. *History*, p. 136.

19. Observe this comment from one of our subtler historians—a comment that comes after an inquiry into the "style" of past masters: "This pressure toward objectivity is realistic because the objects of the historian's inquiry are precisely that, objects, out there in a real and single past. Historical controversy in no way compromises their ontological integrity. The tree in the woods of the past fell in only one way, no matter how fragmentary or contradictory the reports of its fall, no matter whether there are no historians, one historian, or several contentious historians in its future to record and debate it." Peter Gay, *Style in History* (New York, 1974), p. 210. Witness also Gordon Wood's recent call for a born-again positivism: "It is precisely because ever-widening circles of our culture are casting doubt on this traditional epistemology [of nineteenth-century positivism] that historians feel more humble about what they do. Some of the most eminent working historians such as G. R. Elton and Oscar Handlin know that ultimately there can be no alternative for their craft than this old-fashioned epistemology. Historians, warns Elton, 'require not the new humility preached in the wake of Heisenberg, but some return to the assurance of the nineteenth century that the work they are doing deals with reality.' 'The historian's vocation,' writes Handlin, 'depends on this minimal operational article of faith: Truth is absolute; it is absolute as the world is real.' This faith may be philosophically naive, may even be philosophically absurd in this skeptical and relativist-minded age; nevertheless, it is what makes history writing possible. Historians who cut loose from this faith do so at the peril of their discipline." *New York Review of Books*, December 16, 1982, p. 59.

Important differences of outlook in the profession certainly remain, and they still tend to be expressed in terms of relations with the social sciences. The debate is more temperate and constructive now. It usually presupposes a pluralistic appreciation of the many varieties of history and of social science; and hardly anyone denies that part of the contemporary culture with which historians interrogate the past resides in the social sciences. The issue goes rather to the nature of historical and scientific argument. . . . Some historians, in the positivistic tradition, still regard explanation—the testing of general laws by application to specific events—as the sole model of historical explanation. . . . Against this view others contend that the historian is essentially a dramatist, whose narrative logic can never be simplified by any general theories and whose real task is to grasp the unanalyzable complexity of things. Most historians occupy a position somewhere between these extremes: undaunted by the openness and imprecision of historical discourse, yet glad to have the help of any systematic concepts that can offer partial clarification of a particular historical problem. Most would probably agree with H. Stuart Hughes that "the historian's supreme technical virtuosity lies in fusing the new method of social and psychological analysis with his traditional storytelling function."[20]

Yet H. Stuart Hughes's recent plaint intimates that something must have happened since the early '60s to disrupt the liberal, pragmatic consensus Higham believed had emerged in the profession. In the 1973 re-edition of *The Varieties of History*, Fritz Stern, in the wake of the events of 1968, felt history was in crisis and might well lose its audience:

Is history in crisis again? The answer seems to be yes, and the crisis comes from within and without the historical discipline. To some extent, the sense of crisis within the profession indicates concerns that have often assailed the modern historian: the fragmentation of the field, the disparateness of the new

20. *History*, pp. 137–38.

knowledge, the fading of the great syntheses, the identity of
history in relation to the social sciences. Historians are aware
as well of a growing public indifference to history, born perhaps of a sense that the present is so radically different from the
past that the reconstruction of the past seems only of antiquarian interest. It may be part of our professional and social
predicament that at the very time when historical knowledge is
of critical importance it is in fact neglected.[21]

It is in no sense a derogation of deeply felt experience to observe
that the crisis/complacency syndrome, which emerges with such
frequency in our quotations, is part of a very old set of rhetorically
effective *topoi* that often tend to alternate with one another over
time, partly in response to current events. A pronounced sense of
crisis informs Stephen Graubard's preface to *Historical Studies
Today,* a book that stemmed from two issues of *Daedalus.* But
Graubard finds "it difficult to say" whether the sense of crisis is
justified, and he notes that "not one of the more than two dozen
historians who have written for this volume would appear to share
this view [that the discipline is in crisis], though several are critical
of the scholarship in their respective fields."[22] The contributors
tend to judge scholarship on strictly scholarly criteria, and "few
think it is necessary to make excuses for the scholarship of the
1960's."[23] Indeed a bemused air of triumph seems to inform Eric
Hobsbawm's piece on social history, and one is treated to the
curious spectacle of a Marxist discussing a subdiscipline to the
exclusion of its relation to the larger society it purports to study or
to the structure of the historical profession itself. Hobsbawm even
resorts to a ploy Marxists generally associate with a conservative
temperament when he coyly restricts himself to purely objective
analysis of a state of affairs of which he implicitly approves. "This
essay," he tells us, "is an attempt to observe and analyze, not to

21. *Varieties of History* (1956; New York, 1973), p. 9.
22. *Historical Studies Today,* pp. vii–viii.
23. Ibid.

state a personal credo or to express (except where this is clearly stated) the author's preferences and value judgments. I say this at the outset in order to distinguish this essay from others which are defenses of or pleas for the kind of history practiced by their authors—as it happens social history does not need either at the moment."[24] (But Hobsbawm may be toying with the reader, for his essay is indeed truffled with both explicit value judgments and more indirect comments about other approaches and scholars.)

Graubard himself is visibly agitated by the paradoxical coupling of increased professional confidence and decreased public interest in the research of historians. "Many of the developments of recent years have helped those who have viewed history as a science—not a science in the sense that its data may be said to have predictive utility, but a science in François Furet's sense 'of substituting for the elusive "event" of positivist history the regular repetition of data selected or constructed by reason of their compatibility.' History, constructed along such lines, can never serve the purposes of a public that still craves narrative accounts."[25]

"Scientific" history is largely addressed to other historians and, while narrative is in no sense dead, "within the historical profession itself—in the universities of many countries—those who are thought most creative are those who experiment with new methods and new kinds of inquiry. Such historical writing is rarely popular."[26] Graubard seeks a remedy for the divorce between public interest or significance and the demands of professional expertise, but he warns that the turn from "scientific" history cannot mean a return to narrative history of the nineteenth century. He sees a hopeful sign in the study of contemporary events, and he concludes his preface with these words: "If [the historian] succeeds in this [reclaiming the recent past from other fields such as sociology and political science], he will inevitably be led to do

24. Ibid., p. 1.
25. Ibid., p. ix.
26. Ibid.

again what historians from the time of Thucydides were always prepared to do: interpret the contemporary world to their generation."[27]

Graubard's concerns are echoed in subdued fashion in Gilbert's introduction. Gilbert adds a longer-term reason for the crisis in historiography: "The historical process is no longer seen as a continuum. The notion of the continuity of the historical process was Europe-centered. . . . Because of the coherence which this Europe-centered notion of history seemed to possess there could be no doubt about the relevance of the past for the present." Europe was decentered by its loss of power and by the rise to prominence of non-European peoples. For Gilbert the consequences of this phenomenon are clear: "When the past is no longer relevant to the present, occupation with the past becomes antiquarian, a threat that always hangs over the historian's head." Ignoring the question of whether the unqualified postulate of continuity—especially when seen in terms of a dominant position of power—is required for an other than antiquarian interest in the past, Gilbert sees a few promising developments in the "concern for comparative history, for the study of relationships, for the analysis of structure."[28] But he is constrained to conclude his introduction with the rather weak justification that the volume he co-edits may serve to clear up certain misunderstandings in the public about what historians are really doing—although both the preface and the introduction seem to intimate that the direction of professional research is itself one important factor in alienating the general public. Similarly, Gilbert, in his own essay on intellectual history, tries to ward off the hegemony of social history by defining intellectual history in terms of a reduced but more careful and precise variant of traditional *Geistesgeschichte*. Intellectual history can no longer maintain that ideas have a primary causal role in history or even that a *Zeitgeist* rules given periods. It can only make the "modest"

27. Ibid., p. x.
28. Ibid., p. xx.

documentary claim that it "reconstitutes the mind of an individual or of groups at the times when a particular event happened or an advance was achieved."[29] No more basic reconceptualization of intellectual history or its relation to other approaches to history seems feasible in the light of Gilbert's analysis.

With Michael Kammen's edition of *The Past Before Us,* we seem to return to the atmosphere of the volume by Higham, Gilbert, and Krieger. Kammen in his introduction shows qualified but unmistakable signs of optimism about the state of the profession— optimism that is itself perhaps a sign of Kammen's overly generous willingness to see in all other historians the openness to diverse and divergent perspectives that is an admirable trait of his own approach to problems. His magisterially comprehensive survey of recent research is indeed grounds for a sanguine judgment about the condition of the discipline. Not only substantive research but methodological inquiry has proceeded apace. "One result is a discipline that is more responsive to the pluralistic and increasingly egalitarian society in which it functions. A second result, we hope, will be a more cosmopolitan discipline in a shrinking world—a world that is rapidly discovering just how interdependent its past, present, and future prospects are."[30] Thus heightened responsiveness and the promise of cosmopolitanism have accompanied renascent ties with a broader public. And the demands of critics who bemoaned the lack of theoretical self-consciousness in historiography have been answered. "No one should complain today, as Hayden V. White did in 1966, about 'a resistance throughout the entire profession to almost any kind of critical self-analysis.'"[31]

But as Kammen enumerates the major developments in the discipline, one begins to doubt whether long-term tendencies have really changed all that much and whether certain basic grievances have been adequately answered. He notes "(1) the apparent shift

29. Ibid., p. 155.
30. *The Past Before Us,* p. 46.
31. Ibid., p. 33.

from descriptive to analytical history; (2) the proliferation of methodological innovations; and (3) the changing relationship of the 'new social history' to other subdisciplines."[32] These were, curiously enough, precisely the shifts that caused concern in Graubard and Gilbert less than a decade earlier. When one turns to the actual essays in the volume, one is hard pressed to decide whether they substantiate Kammen's relatively optimistic assessment, at least in terms of their own approach to issues. For they tend to be immensely erudite bibliographical assessments of the state of research in various subdisciplines, interspersed with evaluations of specific works and with statistical charts whose very principles of selection and organization are not interrogated. There is in general little self-critical inquiry into the premises of the discipline, and often some of its oldest tenets—the postulates of unity, continuity, and mastery of a documentary repertoire—are affirmed in no uncertain terms.[33] If anything, a documentary model of historical understanding seems less open to criticism to the extent that it has become so thoroughly professionalized as a working assumption of the craft. In this respect, one particularly striking feature of the essays in *The Past Before Us* is the paucity of attention paid to the historiographical past "behind" us. The memory of contributors is relatively short, and there are very few references to past masters who date further back than the last generation. Nor are there even index entries for the names of Ranke, Tocqueville, Marx, Michelet, and so forth—a prominent omission when professionalism itself helps to make the index a crucial "tool" of research. By and large, the appraisals of the state of the discipline in this volume, even when they bemoan certain features of professionalism, also tend to illustrate it, especially by not making an informed exchange with the past of the discipline a living component of its self-understanding in the present.

If one looks to the volume edited by Iggers and Parker, the

---

32. Ibid., pp. 28–29.
33. See, for example, pp. 50, 109, 371, and 504.

impression of heightened professionalism is for the most part confirmed—in spite of the fact that contributors tend at times to be less well established notables in the field. Parker's own concluding essay is an unrestrained, almost Platonic expression of the dream of a total history as a "moving synthesis" across time. In his introduction, Iggers asserts in more lapidary fashion:

> There is a broad diversity in history writing. To be sure among all professional historians there are certain communalities. For all of them history is a reality-seeking enterprise. They seek to discover what happened in human affairs in the past and to understand why it occurred. Ideally, they proceed by canons of scientific research: through critical rational investigation, publication of results, and review by one's peers. Indeed, with respect to procedure, their work has become scientifically ever more rigorous with self-conscious testing of assumptions, concepts, and hypotheses. . . .
> Despite the warnings of such historians as J. H. Hexter, G. R. Elton, Paul Veyne, and Hayden White against the adoption of any scientific, even social-scientific model, for historical inquiry, and White's insistence that history is an intellectual enterprise akin to rhetoric or poetry, historians have become more committed than ever to the scientific ideal of history as a methodologically and conceptually rigorous discipline.[34]

In the first essay of the volume, Louis Mink attempts to stress the specific nature of narrative in contrast to earlier causal and "covering law" models of scientific explanation. Developments in the theory of narrative, Mink tells us, "converge toward an increasing tendency to regard narrative structure as incorporating and communicating a primary and irreducible type of cognitive understanding, and one typically if not uniquely appropriate to historical knowledge. There is also a conceptual connection between the understanding of rational action and narrative as the formulation and expression of such understanding."[35] Yet Mink's own discus-

34. *International Handbook of Historical Studies*, pp. 6, 8.
35. Ibid., p. 25.

sion would seem implicitly to confirm Iggers's introductory comments in that it renders problematic the idea that narrative and
analytic-causal approaches offer basically different or opposed
options in historiography. For the non-reducibility of narrative to
analytic-causal models or "covering laws" seems to be a formal
point that does not affect the comparability of the two ways of
structuring facts as cognitive modes understood in documentary
terms. One has two different forms for arranging or "coding" the
same facts, and narrative codes or structures are themselves to be
objects of theoretical apprehension in the science of narratology.

One need not deny the interest of this approach to narrative to
observe that it does not address features of narration that might
connect with "rhetorical" issues and lead to a broader understanding of cognition. Nor need one slight the importance in historiography of Hayden White, whose work Mink justly sees as the
culmination of the tendency to view historical understanding in
terms of narrative, to observe that White both stressed the role of
rhetoric and threatened to subordinate it to relatively confined
documentary, logical, and dialectical models of cognition. On one
level, White's theory of the figural origins of historical knowledge
reversed ordinary scientific preconceptions in a manner that produced a potentially beneficial shock effect and reopened questions
that seemed to be closed. But, on another level, his theory remained
within the same general frame of reference as the "scientific" views
it turned upside-down. Indeed the informing principle of White's
theory of tropes as the foundation of rhetoric and narrative was a
generative structuralism that presented one level of discourse (the
"tropical") as determinative in the last instance. And his ultimate
appeal in interpretation has been to the role of codes in relation to
which texts or actual uses of language are tokens or instances.
Thus he provided a structuralist analogue of the very "covering
law" model he criticized in causal theories of explanation. But if
the historian in the present was constrained by codes or structures,
his or her relation to the past was extremely permissive. The
problem of subjective relativism in White's "poetics" of histo-

riography stemmed from a neo-idealist and formalist conception of the mind of the historian as a free shaping agent with respect to an inert, neutral documentary record (itself something like a cultural analogue of Kant's "sensuous manifold"). This view tended to obscure both the way people in the past lived, told, and wrote "stories" and the way the documentary record is itself always textually processed before any given historian comes to it. Historians in this sense are confronted with phenomena that pose resistances to their shaping imagination and that present complex problems for their attempt to interpret and reconstruct the past.[36]

By the conventions of the genre and the sweep of my own peroration, I am now constrained to offer my prognosis or "positive" program accompanied by the appropriate hortatory injunctions. I shall live up to this expectation only in a tentative and provisional manner.

How may the necessary components of a documentary model without which historiography would be unrecognizable be conjoined with rhetorical features in a broader, "interactive" understanding of historical discourse? First, I would stress that if rhetoric cannot be entirely subordinated to a restricted scientific model, neither should it be construed in purely instrumental, much less propagandistic, terms. Rhetoric as a mere means to preconceived ends—in brief as a linguistic technology—is itself a reduced modern variant of the more traditional idea of a collection of

36. For a more extensive appraisal of White's work, which attempts to bring out more fully the force of his critique of traditional historiography, see my "Poetics of Historiography: Hayden White's *Tropics of Discourse*" in *Rethinking Intellectual History: Texts, Contexts, Language* (Ithaca, N.Y., 1983). See also the contributions in *History and Theory* XIX, Beiheft 19 (1980). In his "Method and Ideology in Intellectual History: The Case of Henry Adams" (included in *Modern European Intellectual History: Reappraisals and New Perspectives*), White selects ideology rather than tropes as the determinative level in discourse, and he complicates his model by focusing on the role of code-switching. But his emphasis remains on codes in the analysis of usage and texts. White's "The Question of Narrative in Contemporary Theory" (*History and Theory* 23 (1984): 1–33) provides a critical survey of theories of narrative in contemporary thought. This ground-breaking essay indicates how White's own recent work goes beyond the genetic structuralism that appeared in his earlier writing.

strategies and tactics to assure persuasion of another in the pursuit of narrowly self-interested goals. This conception removes rhetoric from any larger notion of sociocultural criticism and political transformation by accepting the invidious definition of it fostered by an absolute, transcendent idea of "truth." With this initial caveat in mind, I would offer the following observations about rhetoric in its bearing upon historiography.

(1) Rhetoric involves a dialogical understanding of discourse and of "truth" itself in contrast to a monological idea of a unified authorial voice providing an ideally exhaustive and definitive (total) account of a fully mastered object of knowledge. Historiography is dialogical in that, through it, the historian enters into a "conversational" exchange with the past and with other inquirers seeking an understanding of it. The problem is the nature of the conversation. Historians generally recognize that they begin not with a "virgin" historical record but with a record processed by the accounts of other historians. But they often tend to reduce their role to the "revision" of standard accounts on the basis of new facts unearthed from the record. This restricted view obscures the strangeness of a dialogue with the dead who are reconstructed through their "textualized" remainders, and it resists any broader reconceptualization of the nature of historical understanding in terms of the interaction between "documentary" knowledge and "rhetorical" exchange. It also underplays the way the "voice" of the historian may be internally "dialogized" when it undergoes the appeal of different interpretations, employs self-critical reflection about its own protocols of inquiry, and makes use of modes such as irony, parody, self-parody, and humor, that is, double- or multiple-voiced uses of language. In this respect, the concept of the dialogical situates that of persuasion in a larger discursive context. Within this context, a "conversation" with the past involves the historian in argument and even polemic—both with others and within the self—over approaches to understanding that are bound up with institutional and political issues.

(2) Rhetoric includes "performative" uses of language that

make a difference in one's relation to the object of study. This does not mean that the historian is obliged to resort to explicit moral judgments, overt didacticism in drawing lessons, or "show and tell" sessions in which one's values or autobiographical propensities are bared to one's audience. The more direct forms of public exposure generally serve a purgative function and rarely inform an account in a telling or transformative way. Instead the "performative" use of language that is effective in shaping discourse raises the question of the way an actual use of language is worked over by certain concerns in making a claim on, and evoking a response from, the listener or reader. Among these concerns is care in putting forth or recognizing the better argument which derives its force from its critical rationality. The role of the aleatory and the absence of absolute certainty do not eliminate this concern, but they do heighten the self-critical demands of rationality, and they serve to check peremptory arrogance in argument. A performative use of language should also involve both historian and addressee in a process of significant change by moving them to respond to the proferred account and its implications for the existing context of interpretation. More generally, rhetorical considerations underscore the political involvements of all interpretation; even the seemingly disinterested description or analysis of facts, disengaged from more manifest ideological functions it may have served in the past (for example, in documenting the rise of the nation-state and/or illustrating the sublime intervention of God in history), nonetheless approximates a neutralist political position. This position may at certain times seem sensible for a group in a weak or easily exposed condition; it remains one position among others and not the simple absence of a position or "bias." But, instead of licensing free variations on the past, variations whose only justification is their furtherance of a present policy, the rhetorical dimension of historiography may rather serve to test current views by requiring the historian to listen attentively to possibly disconcerting "voices" of the past and not simply project narcissistic or self-interested demands upon them.

(3) Rhetoric highlights the problem of how one reads texts. It even raises the question of whether historians are trained to read. I have already noted the tendency of professional historians to see texts as documents in the narrow sense of the word and, by the same token, to ignore the textual dimensions of documents themselves, that is, the manner in which documents "process" or rework material in ways intimately bound up with larger sociocultural and political processes. Historians often read texts as simple sources of information on the level of content analysis. We tend to identify a text directly with what it seems to represent or say—with its propositions, themes, or characterizations. In so doing, we often reduce all texts in homogeneous fashion to mere symptoms of some encompassing phenomenon or process. Indeed we may treat all literature (when literature and philosophy are not eliminated from the relevant historical record) as ordinary pamphlet literature and discuss it solely as a "sign of the times" or in terms of its immediate functions and impact on other, more "tangible" events. Rarely do historians see significant texts as important events in their own right that pose complex problems in interpretation and have intricate relations to other events and to various pertinent contexts. Nor are we inclined to raise the more "rhetorical" question of how texts do what they do—how, for example, they may situate or frame what they "represent" or inscribe (social discourses, paradigms, generic conventions, stereotypes, and so forth). The multiple roles of tropes, irony, parody, and other "rhetorical" devices of composition and arrangement generate resistances to the construal of texts in terms of their "representational" or narrowly documentary functions, and they disclose how texts may have critical or even potentially transformative relations to phenomena "represented" in them. In more subtle fashion, they also point to internal contestations or ways texts differ from themselves in their functioning and interaction with contexts, for texts in variable ways may combine symptomatic, critical, and more "undecidable" relations to given signifying practices and sociocultural processes.

(4) Rhetoric exceeds not only documentary or referential but all utilitarian, workaday, and instrumental functions of language. It involves verbal display or performance in a sense larger than that comprised in the standard notion of the "performative." This ostentatious quality of certain uses of language may be seen as the discursive analogue of the process of gift-giving as analyzed by anthropologists such as Marcel Mauss. Like the gift, rhetorical usage has the quality of being both deeply gratifying and threatening or anxiety-producing, notably with reference to scientific criteria of meaning (such as univocal definition of terms). It also provides a larger setting for the role of tropes as turns of language that manifest a playful and sometimes uncanny potential. (In Paul de Man's hyperbolic formulation: "Rhetoric radically suspends logic and opens up vertiginous possibilities of referential aberration.")[37] In addition, the festive, indeed the carnivalesque side of language reinstates the importance of the epideictic as a mode of praise-abuse that cannot be entirely subordinated to the more "serious" imperatives of the deliberative and forensic modes of argument.[38]

(5) Rhetoric engages the dialectic of recognition among speakers, of which certain forms of persuasion are only the monological

37. *Allegories of Reading,* p. 10. One should note that de Man here refers to possibilities, and the danger in his own approach is the conversion of possibility into necessity by a reduction of rhetoric to the level of an involuted technology of tropes as well as by an almost obsessive, highly predictable tendency to turn the aporia into the hidden agenda or *telos* of language. The risk of referential aberration then paradoxically loses its aleatory status, and aporia threatens to become the *ne plus ultra* of discourse. But to pose problems in these deceptively simple terms is of course to ignore the challenge of de Man's textual practice as well as the force of his rendition of *De docta ignorantia.*

38. "Contemporary scholars betray a certain unease with epideictic as a category. Many list it dutifully as one of the ancient forms of public address, but then pass on quickly to deliberative and forensic oratory, leaving the impression that epideictic is an after-thought meant to cover those orations that are unable to fit neatly into one of the two major classifications. If dealt with at all epideictic orations are characterized as ceremonial or ritualistic showpieces, 'playful exercises by oratorical virtuosos.'" Lawrence W. Rosenfield, "The Practical Celebration of Epideictic," in *Rhetoric in Transition,* ed. Eugene E. White (University Park and London, 1980), p. 131.

variants. It also fosters the awareness that a dialogical relation to the past encounters the problem of coming to terms with "transference" in the psychoanalytic sense of a repetition/displacement of the "object" of study in one's own discourse about it—a problem that is circumvented or repressed *both* in the idea of full empathetic communion with the past *and* in the idea of a totally objective representation of it. One seeks one's own voice in using language "rhetorically," but one also encounters the challenge of other voices of the past, the present, and even the future. Indeed one confronts larger problems in the constitution and functioning of the body politic. It is evident that recognition does not exclude argument, debate, and polemic, nor is it necessarily adjusted to the goal of merging in a single unified voice. It may rather come with a dialogical understanding of discourse that relates unifying and contestatory or disseminating tendencies in language use. One may also seek to retrieve or recover underemphasized aspects of the past and enter them into a more engaging "contest" with tendencies prominent in the present, including the ideal of documentary knowledge itself. In this respect, a vital task of historiography would be to reread its so-called founding fathers with a sensitivity to those sides of their texts that have been obscured, misinterpreted, or underplayed, often because of the documentary or narrowly "scientific" grid through which they are perceived. Marx's strongly carnivalized style, Tocqueville's ironic poise, Michelet's understanding of historical language as a funeral rite, and Carlyle's explosive mixture of modes (one thinks of that uproarious Menippean satire, *Sartor Resartus*) would call for reconsideration in this regard, as would the "styles" of other past masters who are too easily labeled (utopian, scientific, romantic, and so forth) in a manner that is not altogether wrong but that may be highly partial.[39]

39. One historian who was acutely aware of these problems and whose style enacted that awareness was Pieter Geyl. See especially his *Debates with Historians* (Cleveland and New York, 1958). See also Roland Barthes, *Michelet par lui-même* (Paris, 1954); Robert Canary and Henry Kozicki, eds., *The Writing of History*

(6) Rhetoric raises the issues of ambivalence and role tension in language use and their relation to the interaction of discursive modes. With respect to historiography, one obvious problem is the relation between a sympathetic rendering of the past, requiring a measure of identification, and critical distance from it in the interest of both scientific objectivity and critical judgment. A parallel problem is the role of the rhetorical in making all history a living memory that may (as Michelet desired) resurrect the dead and disclose their significance for the present and future. These problems indicate that historiography is itself a tensely mixed mode of language use involving both documentary or "scientific" knowledge and rhetoric in a broader and unavoidably problematic notion of cognition. The possibility that rhetoric may overwhelm familiar but fragile scientific procedures creates understandable anxiety, for if the recent past has taught us anything, it is that standard scientific procedures in evaluating evidence and testing hypotheses are all too easily jeopardized. Rhetorical power that rides roughshod over the demands of empirical accuracy and rigorous proof may at times be more objectionable than complacent business as usual. But, to be scientific, a discursive practice must recognize its own limits as well as the fact that those limits must sometimes be exceeded or even radically transformed. The recognition of limits is not a simple matter of establishing an unbreachable boundary that excludes, or even entails the scapegoating of, some "other" because of its potential abuses. Any powerful force may be abused, and the possibility of abuse would

---

(Madison, Wis., 1978); Lionel Gossman, "Augustin Thierry and Liberal Historiography," *History and Theory* XV, Beiheft 15 (1976) and *The Empire Unpossess'd: An Essay on Gibbon's "Decline and Fall"* (Cambridge, 1981); Dominick LaCapra, "Reading Marx: The Case of *The Eighteenth Brumaire*," "Bakhtin, Marxism, and the Carnivalesque," and "Marxism and Intellectual History," in *Rethinking Intellectual History: Texts, Contexts, Language* (Ithaca, N.Y., 1983); and Linda Orr, *Jules Michelet: Nature, History, and Language* (Ithaca, N.Y., 1976). It would be inexcusable not to mention the works of Kenneth Burke, which touch upon all of the problems I have evoked. Needless to say, the list of names and texts in this note could be extended considerably.

be enough to disqualify any unsettling—and enlivening—current in existence.

(7) The lack of attention to the problem of rhetoric, or the simple dichotomy between science and rhetoric, induces a tendency to perceive rhetoric as "merely" rhetorical and to understand scientific truth in terms of a rather blind rhetoric of anti-rhetoric. This tendency, which defines science as the adversary or antithesis of rhetoric, has often been conjoined with a defense of a "plain style" that attempts or pretends to be entirely transparent to its object. It is not uncommon to observe that the anti-rhetoric of plain style or, more elaborately, of "scientificity" is itself a self-denying quest for a certain rhetoric, a rhetoric unadorned by figures, unmoved by emotion, unclouded by images, and universalistic in its conceptual or mathematical scope. It is less common to construe this quest in a self-reflexive way that raises the question of the rhetoric of transparency in coming to terms with certain issues. For this quest may be as dubious in its intellectual foundations as it is in its sociopolitical implications. It may also further a one-sided effort to elaborate a science of rhetoric rather than an art of rhetorical usage, a science that presents usage purely and simply as a precipitate (or instantiation) of structures and codes. Indeed one of the most fateful turns in the teaching of rhetoric is that from a pedagogy of emulation of exempla (poems, parodies, satires, and so forth) to a codification of terminology and principles. The renewal of the problem of rhetoric may make possible a better understanding of the complex relationship between codes and usage with respect not only to the past but to the historian's own discourse. It may thus provide greater insight into the liminal position of the historian's craft between "science" and "art"—a position that cannot be fixated once and for all precisely because it calls for recurrent reconceptualization.

(8) It must be actively recognized that any attempt to link rhetoric and a "dialogical" relation to the past, including my own, would be hopelessly ideological if it did not indicate its limits and the problem of transforming them. Any "dialogue" with the past

in professional historiography takes place in a larger social, political, economic, and cultural context that places severe restrictions upon it. One prominent feature of this discursive and institutional context in the modern period has been a marked split between (and within) elite and popular cultures accompanied by the emergence of a commodified "mass culture" or "culture industry" that has alienated certain cultural elites and threatened to appropriate both older and newer forms of popular culture. Even attempts within elite culture to appeal to popular modes (e.g., the carnivalesque) in order to contest an invasive culture industry and its processes of commodification have often occurred within experimental forms that are inaccessible to popular groups and frequently consumed by privileged classes as status symbols. This long-term problem provides the setting for the more superficial fluctuations in the crisis/complacency syndrome in historiography that I have charted and that will no doubt continue their course in the future.[40] Without a self-critical attempt to come to terms with its own insertion in this setting—a setting that Gramsci would have seen as posing the question of hegemony—even the most insistent "dialogue" with the past is condemned to be a dead letter.

This essay as a whole may be read as an oblique commentary on my epigraph, which is taken from Machiavelli's famous letter to his friend, the ambassador Francesco Vettori. With the defeat of his beloved Florentine republic, Machiavelli had fallen from his position of power and from grace, and he was anxious to reinstate himself in an actively political role. The quotation which serves as my epigraph prefaced Machiavelli's announcement that he had

40. In his epilogue to a republication of his section of the book, John Higham sees the present as a "time of troubles." He continues to hold out consensus on a research paradigm as an ideal in historiography, but he now finds it elusive given sociopolitical events, "intrusions from other academic disciplines" (p. 242), and debates within the historical profession itself. He provides little sense that a "time of troubles" may also be read as a time for basic reconceptualization of the discipline. (*History: Professional Scholarship in America* [Baltimore and London, 1983].)

spent his time in exile writing a work that ought to be welcome to a
prince, especially to a new prince. He dedicated *The Prince* to
Florence's new ruler, Guiliano de'Medici, whose favor he hoped to
win. The story that relates its genesis in a realistic myth of origins
may be taken to emblematize the situation of historiography and
related "human sciences" as complex modes of discourse in which
an exchange with the past is always bound up with a present
dialogue.[41] And the vestimentary ritual with which Machiavelli
clothed his own dialogues with the dead may be read as a sign that
political discourse, while always enmeshed in problems of power
and interest, may also open itself to broader currents that test and
contest the limits of a conventional understanding of both politics
and discourse.

41. In an unpublished essay ("*Per miei carmi:* Machiavelli's Discourses of
Exile"), John Najemy subtly shows how the discussion of politics as a discourse of
mastery was at times playfully intertwined, in the letters between Machiavelli and
Vettori, with a discussion of love and the impolitic loss of control it often brought.
One may also consult Nancy S. Struever's excellent work, *The Language of
History in the Renaissance: Rhetoric and Historical Consciousness in Florentine
Humanism* (Princeton, 1970).

2

The Cheese and the Worms:
The Cosmos of a
Twentieth-Century Historian

... in wanting (at a distance which is the remoteness of
double reflection) to read solo the original text of the
individual, human existence-relationship, the old text,
well known, handed down from the fathers—to read it
through yet once more, if possible in a more heartfelt
way.

> Søren Kierkegaard, "A First and Last Declaration,"
> *Concluding Unscientific Postscript*

Then they urged him to talk, and Menocchio threw
caution to the wind.

> Carlo Ginzburg, *The Cheese and the Worms*

IN 1983, I spent the last days of December in Ithaca, New York. I
would have preferred a place offering a more temperate climate.
Seeking shelter from the inquisitorial rigor of an especially harsh
winter, I found my thoughts turning once again to a topic that has
tended to preoccupy me in the recent past: the state of contemporary historiography. Metahistorical commentary can itself be a
bone-chilling affair. It is a process of double reflection, twice-
removed from the ostensible object of the historian's quest—a

process that makes the immediacy of past experience seem especially remote. How can such a seemingly inhuman enterprise enable one to read old texts, indeed the text of existence itself, in a more heartfelt way? I would much prefer to devote my time and energy to more congenial, indeed storylike matters—perhaps to rummage in rich deposits of archival papers and to tell their tales in ingratiatingly narrative forms. But, leafing through the pages of recent historical works, I come upon claims that capture my curiosity and configurations of ideas that challenge my understanding. At times, I almost seem to be in another world.

Historiography today is not in that state of fermentation to be found in fields such as literary criticism and Continental philosophy. Historians tend to pride themselves on their immunity to the wormlike doubt and self-reflective scrutiny that have appeared in other areas of inquiry, notably those infiltrated by recent French thought. Far from seeing recent critical initiatives as holding forth the angelic promise of a reformation or even a renaissance in historical studies, many historians have been seized with what might almost be called a counter-reformational zeal in reasserting orthodox procedures. But the contemporary historical profession is not a solid block, and even the most traditional scholars show an openness to at least a few newer movements. If one were to generalize somewhat rashly about prominent trends in the profession, one might list the following: an inclination to rely on a social definition of context as an explanatory matrix; a shift toward an interest in popular culture; a reconceptualization of culture in terms of collective discourses, mentalities, world views, and even "languages"; a redefinition of intellectual history as the study of social meaning as historically constituted; and an archivally based documentary realism that treats artifacts as quarries for facts in the reconstitution of societies and cultures of the past. These trends are in many significant ways progressive in comparison with earlier practices, but they may become dubious when they engender dogmatic sociocentrism, methodological populism, the refusal to recognize the historical significance of exceptional aspects of culture, and an oversimplified understanding of language and meaning frequently attended by a reductive use of texts and documents.

A recent book which, I think, embodies both the promise and the dangers of contemporary trends has captured the historical imagination: Carlo Ginzburg's *The Cheese and the Worms*.[1] It is rare for such a small book (128 pages of principal text, 15 of preface, 43 of notes) to make such large waves in the profession. Ginzburg's translators accurately observe: "The book has been rightly hailed as one of the most significant recent contributions to a burgeoning field of study, the popular culture of early modern Europe" (p. viii). Roger Chartier gives a more extensive account of why the book has attracted notice:

> As Carlo Ginzburg shows us, when the documents authorize it, it is entirely permissible to explore, as through a magnifying glass, the way a man of the people can think and use the sparse intellectual elements that reach him from literate culture by means of his books and the reading he gives them. Here Bakhtin is turned upside down, since a system of representations is constructed from fragments borrowed from scholarly and bookish culture, giving them another meaning because in the system's foundation there is another culture: "Behind the books pondered by Menocchio we have discovered a reading code; and behind this code, a whole stratum of oral culture." We cannot then postulate as necessary the connection established by Felix Gilbert, between the social broadening of the field of research in intellectual history and the recourse to statistical procedure. In fact, if under certain conditions the quantitative approach (internal or external) to the most elaborate texts can be accepted as legitimate, conversely, when the archives permit it, the intellectual work of the most anonymous of readers may be amenable to the analytical procedures ordinarily reserved for the "greatest" thinkers.[2]

1. *The Cheese and the Worms*, trans. John and Anne Tedeschi (Baltimore, 1980), first pub. in Italian in 1976. All page references are to this edition.

2. "Intellectual History or Sociocultural History? The French Trajectories," in Dominick LaCapra and Steven L. Kaplan, eds., *Modern European Intellectual History: Reappraisals and New Perspectives* (Ithaca, 1982), pp. 35–36.

Thus Ginzburg, through an imaginative variant of research into the response of a reader, has revealed a mode of qualitative social history that presumably employs techniques of "high" or "elite" intellectual history. In the process, he opens to us the "cosmos" of a sixteenth-century miller, the unforgettable Domenico Scandella, called Menocchio. Although I am qualified neither by field nor by period specialization, I would like to attempt at least a partial reading of Ginzburg's text—a text that is itself to some significant extent emblematic of the "cosmos" of the twentieth-century historian. The similitude between Ginzburg's *The Cheese and the Worms* vis-à-vis the contemporary historical profession and Menocchio's "world view" vis-à-vis sixteenth-century popular culture is of course far from complete. While Ginzburg's remarkable book has received widespread acclaim, not all historians praising it would agree with all aspects of its argument, even if they might assent to its general conception of the direction in which historical research should go. For another thing, for Ginzburg we have a written text while for Menocchio we have only a putative "world view" pieced together inferentially on the basis of two inquisition registers. (The trials were separated by fifteen years, and as an old man, Menocchio was burned at the stake.)

A recurrent motif of Ginzburg's book is the significance of discrepancies between what occurs in the texts Menocchio read and the active, indeed aggressive readings of them Menocchio offered. Ginzburg interprets these symptomatic discrepancies as indications of an oral, popular (more specifically, peasant) culture that unconsciously served as the grid or filter for Menocchio's readings. I would like to point to a discrepancy between the role of this interpretation in the dominant argument of Ginzburg's principal text and what tends to surface at times in his two prefaces (one to the English translation and the other to the Italian edition), in one important footnote, and in fleeting remarks throughout the text that are expanded in an almost explosively forceful crescendo toward the end of the principal text. This discrepancy indicates an important tension in Ginzburg's conception of what Menocchio stands for and, more generally, in his account of the relations among popular, high, and dominant culture in the sixteenth century and over time. One may initially formulate this tension in terms of the contrast between an idea of the autonomy of popular culture and an idea of its reciprocal or circular interaction with dominant or hegemonic culture. We shall come to see the inadequacy of this initial formulation, but it attests to the strength of Ginzburg's commitment to a conception of popular culture that, if not autonomous, is primordial or fundamental in the "cosmos" of Menocchio.

Let us begin with the argument that appears dominant in the principal text, at least until its concluding pages. It presents oral, popular, peasant culture as a very old, fundamentally pre-Christian phenomenon which the turmoil of the Reformation allowed to surface and to break through the crust of more visible cultural forms. Ginzburg shares this vision with Mikhail Bakhtin, and his innovation is to present it as the oral "code" that shapes Menocchio's reading of written texts. Here is one of Ginzburg's typical formulations of his view:

> What did a cosmogony such as the one described by Menocchio—the primordial cheese from which the worm-angels are produced—have to do with the Reformation? How can one trace back to the Reformation statements such as those attributed to Menocchio by his fellow villagers: "everything that we see is God, and we are gods," "the sky, earth, sea, air, abyss, and hell, all is God"? Provisionally, it's best to attribute them to a substratum of peasant beliefs, perhaps centuries old, that were never wholly wiped out. By breaking the crust of religious unity, the Reformation indirectly caused these old beliefs to emerge; the Counter-Reformation, attempting to restore unity, brought them into the light of day in order to sweep them away.

On the basis of this hypothesis, then, Menocchio's radical statements will not be explained by tracing them to Anabaptism or, worse yet, to a generic 'Lutheranism.' Rather, we should ask if they don't belong within an autonomous current

of peasant radicalism, which the upheaval of the Reformation
had helped to bring forth, but which was much older. (pp. 20–
21)

In the course of the book, the attribution of Menocchio's "world
view" to an oral popular culture or peasant radicalism (here explicitly termed "autonomous") becomes much more than an "hypothesis" in either the scientific or the ordinary sense. Scientifically, Ginzburg's interpretation (as he will acknowledge in the
footnote we have yet to discuss) cannot be proved in accordance
with standard criteria of verification and falsification. I would,
however, accept the status of the view as an "hypothesis" in the
more ordinary sense. It is quite plausible to argue that Menocchio's
ideas had a significant relation to oral, popular traditions of indeterminate age. Still moot, however, would be the nature of the
relationship between these oral traditions and other aspects or
levels of culture. Equally moot would be their role in comparison
with other factors and forces in Menocchio's reading of written
texts and his interaction with other aspects of culture.

Part of the attraction of Bakhtin's conception of an age-old,
popular, oral culture is the fact that—despite his periodic invoca-
tions of a phonocentric metaphysic—he leaves its status relatively
"hypothetical" (in the ordinary sense), does not routinize or place
excessive "scientific" freight upon it, and uses it rhetorically to
motivate often insightful interpretations.[3] Ginzburg, however, demands more of the conception he adapts from Bakhtin, and he
attempts to resolve moot issues in a particular direction. For him,
an oral, popular, peasant culture, seen either as autonomous or at
least as primordial and fundamental, is *the* key to Menocchio's
readings and his "world view." All the metaphors Ginzburg employs assume the foundational status of oral culture in Menocchio's "cosmos." One has archaeological and arboreal metaphors,

---

3. On Bakhtin, see Dominick LaCapra, "Bakhtin, Marxism, and the Carnivalesque," in *Rethinking Intellectual History: Texts, Contexts, Language*
(Ithaca, 1983), pp. 291–324.

at times mixed to indicate the incontestably privileged status of oral, popular culture, for example, in a phrase such as "a deeply-rooted current of peasant radicalism brought to the surface by the Reformation" (p. 33). And in a note we are told that Ginzburg chooses the term "peasant radicalism" in line with "Marx's phrase, according to which radicalism 'grasps things at the roots,' an image that, after all, is singularly appropriate to the present context" (p. 143n). One also finds ocular metaphors: "More than the text, then, what is important is the key to his reading, a screen that he unconsciously placed between himself and the printed page: a filter that emphasized certain words while obscuring others, that stretched the meaning of a word, taking it out of context, that acted on Menocchio's memory and distorted the very words of the text. And this screen, this key to his reading, continually leads us back to a culture that is very different from the one expressed on the printed page—one based on an oral tradition" (p. 33).

Ginzburg's own obsessive metaphors lead us as his readers to his own strong investments in the idea of a primordial, oral, popular culture—investments that are metaphysical, literary, and methodological.

Metaphysically, Ginzburg elaborates the binary opposition between speech and writing in terms reminiscent of Claude Lévi-Strauss in a chapter entitled "A Writing Lesson" in *Tristes Tropiques*.[4] In so doing, he indulges in a phonocentrism that makes a scapegoat of writing and represses in speech itself the characteristics projected exclusively onto writing. In Ginzburg's words:

> He [Menocchio] had experienced in his person the historic leap of incalculable significance that separates the gesticulated, mumbled, shouted speech of oral culture from that of written culture, toneless and crystallized on the page. The first is almost an extension of the body, the second "a thing of the mind." The victory of written over oral culture has been, principally, a victory of the abstract over the empirical. In the

4. *Tristes Tropiques* (1955; New York, 1974), chap. 28, pp. 294–304.

possibility of finding release from particular situations one has
the root of the connection that has always indissolubly bound
writing and power. . . . He understood that the written word,
and the ability to master and to transmit written culture, were
sources of power. . . . (p. 59)

Thus the authority of Menocchio's putative experience is invoked
to authenticate the spoken word and to relegate writing to the
suspect sphere of power—the resource of hegemonic or dominant
culture. The general ruses involved in a phonocentric metaphysic,
with its relation to a myth of lost origins, have been so thoroughly
"deconstructed" by Jacques Derrida that it is superfluous to repeat
that gesture here.5 (Ginzburg does mention Derrida in the preface
to the Italian edition, but it is only to dismiss as "facile" and
"nihilistic" his criticisms of Foucault's *Histoire de la folie*—criticisms which Ginzburg seems to have misunderstood.) Suffice it to
note that power is not absent from the spoken word, as the oral
performance of the inquisitors themselves would be enough to
show. Nor is writing invariably an abstract "thing of the mind"—
indeed it is never simply a "thing of the mind." The problem is that
of the variable empirical differences between speech and writing
(as well as between "preliterate" societies and societies in which
speech is supplemented by writing)—a problem whose articulation with reference to specific circumstances and contexts the
metaphysic invoked by Ginzburg readily functions to obscure. For
the historian, the interest of Derrida's extension of the notion of
écriture to encompass both speech and writing (in the ordinary
sense) is to problematize tendentious, universal oppositions between the two and to shift the burden of proof in specific cases to
concrete research. It is perhaps not beside the point to observe that
Menocchio's "experience," as described by Ginzburg himself,
does not lend itself to a phonocentric metaphysic. Menocchio had
a deep respect for books, read them with intensity and passion, and

5. See especially *Of Grammatology*, trans. Gayatri Chakravorty Spivak (1967;
Baltimore, 1976), pt. 2, chap. 1, pp. 101–140.

sought authorization for his views in what he had read. "He had
read only a few books and these largely by chance. He had chewed
upon and squeezed meaning out of every word in these books. He
pondered them for years; for years words and phrases had fer-
mented in his memory" (p. 45). The way Menocchio read might
itself indicate that his choice of books was not as fortuitous as
Ginzburg believes. He had, for example, special regard for a book
that ill accords with the thesis of the primordiality of oral, peasant
culture: the Bible, "a book different from all others because it
contained an essential element provided by God" (p. 31). As we
shall see, however, the point is not simply to reverse Ginzburg's
emphasis and arrive at a picture of a piously bookish Menocchio; it
is rather to question the cogency of simple reversals in general,
whether in favor of popular, oral, peasant culture or in favor of
high, written, hegemonic culture (an excessively simple opposition
postulated, moreover, in series of terms that are not altogether
coincident).

Ginzburg's own idea of the primordial importance of oral
culture in Menocchio's reading and "cosmos" is reinforced by a
structuralist methodology and a reliance on a particular literary
form: the detective story. His narrative is itself strangely anecdotal
and geometrical, projectively empathetic and reductively analytic, extremely fragmented (62 chapters for 128 pages, some chapters only one or two paragraphs long) and overly unified in theme
and thesis. The object of his quest is obviously a deep structure,
and his notion of a privileged code, filter, or grid provides a
convenient reductive device to make full, unified sense of Menocchio's recorded comments. A rather rigid structuralist methodology might itself be seen as the "deep structure" of a "super-
ficially" diffuse and at times unstitched narrative. But, on another
level, the format of the detective story itself assures that the
"whodunit" will reveal a single agent: oral, popular culture. Indeed the fateful convergence of metaphysical, methodological, and
narrative assumptions on a fundamental idea of oral culture creates in the reader the sense that there is a rather blind transferential

relationship between Ginzburg as interpreter and Menocchio as
Ginzburg "reads" him—Menocchio who presumably read "as if
he were searching for confirmation of ideas and convictions that
were already firmly entrenched" (p. 36).

One may note, before inquiring further into the nature of oral,
popular culture in Ginzburg's account, that a structuralist methodology has a paradoxical effect. Ginzburg rightly wants to op-
pose the prejudice that all ideas originally emanate from high
culture or dominant classes—that they come from the "heads of
monks and university professors, certainly not of millers and peasants" (p. 155n). (This prejudice is perhaps less to be opposed, since
opposition invites simple reversal, than to be dismissed as patently
ridiculous.) He wants to show the active nature of Menocchio's
readings. Yet the emphasis upon oral culture as a privileged code
that Menocchio unconsciously employed returns the miller to
passivity on another level, and it reduces to mere superficiality his
strong-mindedness and audacity. To the extent that Menocchio is
a figure of popular culture, it also obscures the fact that there can
be exceptions on the level of popular culture itself. In addition, it
relies on a structural concept (or fixation) of the unconscious as a
grid or filter that unifies experience. It thereby represses the more
challenging and disconcerting "notion" of the unconscious as a
paradoxical name for processes of repression, displacement, and
condensation—processes that bring to the fore the significance of
the problem of the historian's own transferential relation to the
past as well as the need to work through that relation in a critical
and self-critical way. Yet it is this inevitable transferential relation
that discloses in more specific terms how Menocchio is "very close
to us: a man like ourselves, one of us" and how his story "implicitly poses a series of questions for our own culture and for us"
(preface to the English edition, pp. xi–xii).

What is the nature of the oral, popular, peasant culture which I
have repeatedly invoked but left rather mysterious? It must be
confessed that its nature is also rather mysterious in *The Cheese
and the Worms*. The diffuse narrative and anecdotal style facili-

tates the treatment of it in vague, piecemeal, and allusive terms. It is more often invoked than it is described or analyzed, and its clarity is in inverse relation to its putative explanatory power. This fact is perhaps in keeping with the metaphysical dimension of Ginzburg's account, wherein "popular culture" acquires traits usually associated with a "god-term." Matters are not helped when, toward the end of the book, Ginzburg appeals to Scolio's *Settennario* as embodying the somewhat elusive oral tradition, for, although the poem was written by "an unknown rustic," it includes elements of fundamentalist faith in the Ten Commandments, iconoclasm, desire for a plain style, praise of sobriety and piety, a frugal conception of a proper life, an other-worldly idea of utopia, dogmatic intolerance, anti-intellectualism, and an anticarnivalesque animus. (See pp. 112–118.) The fact that the poem was written by "an unknown rustic" raises questions about the unity of popular, oral culture even when the latter is restricted to the peasantry, for that culture was not as homogeneous in its traditions and practices as Ginzburg's references to it suggest. It harbored inner differences and divisions as well as an internalization of aspects of dominant culture, notably Christianity. Ginzburg is of course not ignorant of this point, but it plays very little role in the story he tells. One crucial variant of it will, however, emerge with reference to the figure of Menocchio itself, especially in the light of considerations that are prominent in Ginzburg's concluding pages.

Four characteristics of oral, popular culture seem to emerge as especially significant in the comments dispersed in Ginzburg's account. First, there is a materialism expressed, for example, in Menocchio's cosmogony of cheese and worms and in his questioning of the doctrines of a creator God, the divinity of Christ, the immaculate conception, and the immortality of souls. Here, however, one may note that Menocchio, unlike Ginzburg, does not engage in the quest for a primordial or foundational level of explanation, either by giving priority to oral over written culture or by stipulating some single principle or entity as the first cause of the others. In his variations on the story of how the world was like cheese from which angels and God himself emerged, he is quite flexible, even labile, in discussing the relations of chaos, God, and "the most holy majesty." At one point he argues that "all was chaos . . . and out of that bulk a mass formed—just as cheese is made out of milk—and worms appeared in it, and these were the angels. The most holy majesty decreed that these should be God and the angels" (quoted, p. 53). Here chaos seems primary, and "the most holy majesty," distinguished from God, seems to have the role of an order-giving demiurge. In response to the vicar general's question about the nature of this most holy majesty, Menocchio says that he conceives him as "the spirit of God who was from eternity." Here the spirit of God is coeval with chaos and precedes God. In another version, however, Menocchio makes God eternal and exchanges positions between him and the holy spirit. In answer to the inquisitor's question, Menocchio reportedly answers: "I believe that they were always together, that they were never separated, that is, neither chaos without God, nor God without chaos" (quoted, p. 54). In the face of further inquisitorial questioning, Menocchio asserts that God is eternal with chaos but at first their union is only implicit—"he did not know himself nor was he alive, but later he became aware of himself and this is what I mean that he was made from chaos" (quoted, p. 54). Later in his own account, Ginzburg provides a misleading linear reduction of Menocchio's reported views: "Chaos preceded the 'most holy majesty,' which is not further defined; from chaos came the first living beings—the angels, and God himself who was the greatest among them—by spontaneous generation, 'produced by nature'" (p. 57). One might, by contrast, insist that there is value in Menocchio's more flexible formulations, especially with reference to our own secularized analogue of it: the quest for unified explanations or primordial levels in relation to forces that contest this quest. Ginzburg's own explanatory gestures in this regard may at times be close to the inquisitorial logic that he explicitly rejects.

A second feature of peasant culture is an egalitarianism combined with a view of existing society as divided between "superiors" and "poor people" (p. 16). Menocchio saw ecclesiastical hierarchy as a principal embodiment of oppression because the church was still a large landholder. "Against this enormous edifice built on the exploitation of the poor, Menocchio set forth a very different religion, where all members were equal because the spirit of God was in all of them" (p. 17).

A third feature is tolerance in a positive sense related to the affirmation of "the equivalence of all faiths, in the name of a simplified religion, free of dogmatic or confessional considerations" (p. 51). In Menocchio's reported words: "The majesty of God has given the Holy Spirit to all, to Christians, to heretics, to Turks, to Jews; and he considers them all dear, and they are all saved in the same manner" (quoted, p. 51). Or again: "I believe that each person holds his faith to be right, but we do not know which is the right one" (quoted with emphasis added, p. 51).

Fourth, one has a this-worldly utopianism. "The image of a more just society was consciously projected onto a non-eschatological future. It wasn't the Son of Man high up in the clouds, but men like Menocchio—the peasants of Montereale whom he vainly tried to convince—who, through their struggles, would have to be the bearers of this 'new world'" (p. 86). It is curious that, despite Ginzburg's reliance on Bakhtin and his recognition that "the center of the culture portrayed by Bakhtin is the carnival" (preface to the Italian edition, p. xvi), Ginzburg himself does not elaborate on the actual role of carnival in Montereale or the significance of the fact that one of Menocchio's own occupations—as a guitar player at feasts—could be seen as carnivalesque. Nor does he stress the relation between carnival and utopia. In Bakhtin carnival is the realistic, this-worldly utopia that alternates in variable ways with workaday, "serious" practices, and it characterizes a mode of life in which it is legitimate to have both "serious" and "joking" relations to the same beliefs or institutions. Indeed for Bakhtin things are best when one can joke about what one holds most sacred.

An unavoidable question is whether "a few soundings confirm

the existence of traits reducible to a common peasant culture," as Ginzburg affirms (preface to the Italian edition, p. xxi). To what extent are the four remarkable traits I have extracted from Ginzburg's account unique to peasant culture, originally developed in peasant culture (where at times one even seems to have a popular enlightenment *avant la lettre*), or especially prevalent in peasant culture? Ginzburg does not provide answers to these questions, and he does not even formulate them in sufficiently distinct and differentiated form. He would like to affirm the existence of an age-old oral tradition that is the privileged repository of the traits he sees and admires in Menocchio. But he nonetheless furnishes evidence that in the sixteenth century, the peasants and villagers whom Menocchio "vainly tried to convince" also harbored other tendencies, indeed countercurrents. Not only does their testimony at Menocchio's trials seem to indicate an assimilation of aspects of dominant culture. There also seem to be tendencies in the peasantry that cannot be construed solely as mimetic derivatives or internalizations of the dominant culture, for example, a degree of intolerance toward outsiders. Conversely, it may be argued that the traits ascribed to oral, popular culture did have certain analogues in Christianity, for example, the "materialistic" belief in the resurrection of the body, the egalitarianism of evangelical currents, and the propensity for other-worldly visions of a heavenly utopia to shade into this-worldly protest. Most significantly, perhaps, pre-Reformation Christianity had been relatively tolerant of heterodoxies, too tolerant for reformers who wanted a more rigorous spirituality and might have found it difficult to distinguish between tolerance and abuse. There is a sense in which Menocchio seems, among other things, to be pre-Reformation in his own expansive understanding of Christianity.

These observations raise what is the larger and most pressing question: what were the variable relations over time—including the relation between orthodoxy and heterodoxies—in the interaction among the hegemonic culture(s) of dominant classes, popular culture(s), and high culture(s)? Ginzburg does not explore this question in a sufficiently discriminating way. Indeed he is inhibited from so doing by his insistence upon the role of a unified popular culture as the key to Menocchio's "cosmos" and by his reliance on the binary opposition between dominant and popular culture. In his retrospective preface written for the English edition, he denies the charge that he ascribed "absolute autonomy" to peasant culture and, appealing to Bakhtin, he affirms instead the existence of "circularity": "between the culture of the dominant classes and that of the subordinate classes there existed, in preindustrial Europe, a circular relationship composed of reciprocal influences, which traveled from low to high as well as from high to low. (Exactly the opposite, therefore, of the 'concept of the absolute autonomy and continuity of peasant culture' that has been attributed to me—see notes pp. 154–155)" (p. xi). In the preface to the original Italian edition, there is a somewhat similar remark which also relies on a reference to Bakhtin: "Cultural dichotomy, then—but also a circular, reciprocal influence between the cultures of subordinate and ruling classes that was especially intense in the first half of the sixteenth century" (p. xvii). Yet we have seen that in the principal body of the text, Ginzburg does refer to "an autonomous current of peasant radicalism" (p. 21), and he invests a great deal in the idea of a primordial substratum of peasant beliefs. Toward the end of the principal text, he casts his views in a longer-term historical perspective:

> Such figures as Rabelais and Brueghel probably weren't exceptions. All the same, they closed an era characterized by hidden but fruitful exchanges, moving in both directions between high and popular cultures. The subsequent period was marked, instead, by an increasingly rigid distinction between the culture of the dominant classes and artisan and peasant cultures, as well as by the indoctrination of the masses from above. We can place the break between these two periods in the second half of the sixteenth century, basically coinciding with the intensification of social differentiation under the impulse of the price revolution. But the decisive crisis had occurred a few decades

before, with the Peasants' War and the reign of the Anabaptists
in Münster. At that time, while maintaining and even empha-
sizing the distance between the classes, the necessity of recon-
quering, ideologically as well as physically, the masses threatening to break loose from every sort of control was
dramatically brought home to the dominant classes. (p. 126)

This passage emphasizes the reciprocity or circularity of exchanges in the early sixteenth century, and it sees a "break" in the
second half of the century. But it shifts its terms of comparison
from the relation between "high and popular cultures" in the
earlier period to that between "the culture of the dominant classes
and artisan and peasant cultures" in the later one, as if "high" and
"dominant" were equivalent terms and as if peasants and artisans
could be amalgamated at least in the later period. The terms and
comparisons of the overall argument seem confused and contradictory: an autonomous or at least fundamental tradition of peasant culture is nonetheless in reciprocal or circular relations with a
high (or at times dominant) culture in the early sixteenth century,
and a break supervenes in the later sixteenth century. But how can
a peasant culture be both autonomous (or at least primordial,
fundamental, infrastructural—the key, filter, grid, and so forth)
and involved in reciprocal or circular relations with a dominant
culture? Even at the risk of becoming embroiled in tedious seman-
tic exercises or, even worse, of repeating on Ginzburg's text a
variant of inquisitorial logic, one would like a little more
clarification.

The footnote on pages 154–55—another retrospective addition
to the text—at once adds a glimmer of light and intensifies confusion. Ginzburg again denies the charge of "absolute autonomy"
and affirms circular or reciprocal relations without trying to expli-
cate the relations between (just plain?) autonomy (or at least
primordiality) and reciprocity (allowing perhaps for oxymoronic
"relative" autonomy). He does, however, make this rather surpris-
ing concession: "It's legitimate to object that the hypothesis that
traces Menocchio's ideas about the cosmos to a remote oral tradi-

tion is also unproven—and perhaps destined to remain so . . . even if, as I've stated above, I intend in the future to demonstrate its possibility with additional evidence." He then adds this rather astounding comment: "In any case, it would be advisable to develop new criteria of proof specifically suited to a line of research based on so thoroughly a heterogeneous, in fact unbalanced, documentation. That a new field of investigation alters not only the methods but the very criteria of proofs in a given discipline is shown, for example, in the history of physics: the acceptance of atomic theory has necessitated a change in the standards of evidence that had developed within the sphere of classical physics" (p. 155). I shall return shortly to the question of documentation. But the reference to altered criteria of proof is striking, and the reference to physics seems little more than diversionary. In the text of *The Cheese and the Worms*, it is largely the force of metaphysical desire for a primordial, deep structure in history and in the explanatory efforts of the historian that impels contradictory movements in the argument, and the only alterations in the criteria of proof seem to be in the direction of a secular mythology that, especially in its unacknowledged forms, may have dubious professional implications. A reference to Freud's encounter with the "primal crime" or Lévi-Strauss's admission that, at the limit, he too offers a myth—the myth of mythology—might have been more apposite.

Ginzburg's footnote does make explicit a consideration that, while periodically adumbrated, is not adequately explored in the body of the principal text: hegemony and its import for reciprocity in relations. As he observes, "dominant culture and subordinate culture are matched in an unequal struggle, where the dice are loaded" (p. 155n). One effect of Ginzburg's stress on oral, popular culture as well as of his narrative technique in the principal text is that hegemonic or dominant culture remains a largely residual category, even an image of the radically "other." It is clear enough that the inquisitor can condemn Menocchio to the stake for heresy but that Menocchio cannot punish the inquisitor for intolerant dogmatism and rigid orthodoxy. But we learn little about those who persecute Menocchio or about the relations between religious and secular authorities in a hegemonic structure. Here Ginzburg's empathy with the oppressed induces a piecemeal, evanescent perception of the oppressors, whose own problems, anxieties, and motivations remain covered by a veil of silence.

With reference to the issue of hegemonic culture, one may introduce the problem of documentation in a sense somewhat different from Ginzburg's own. An inquisition register is, as Ginzburg observes, part of the "archives of the repression." He sadly notes in the preface to the Italian edition that the bulk of the evidence we have on popular culture comes from such repositories of hegemonic culture and that the reconstruction of popular beliefs and practices must be inferential and indirect. But his own reflections seem to stop at this point, and his only concern seems to be to find new ways of making inferences about a "reality" he is tempted to construe in metaphysical and mythological terms. In the principal text, the story-line and the analytic format are well in place before there are indications that he is basing them on inquisition registers, and the fact that he is never becomes problematic. And, despite his insistence on the opposition between the oral and the written when it is construed in terms of a questionable metaphysic, he does not address the difficulty posed by the more specific problem of the written inscription of oral testimony by notaries of the inquisition. Nor does he recognize the significance of what might ironically be called *la question préalable*—the need for a close, critical reading of documents such as inquisition registers before they are used as quarries for facts and sources for inferential reconstructions of "reality." For these documents are themselves historical realities that do not simply represent but also supplement the realities to which they refer, and a critical reading of them may provide insight into cultural processes—insight of a sort that at least resists mythologizing desires. For one thing, an inquisition register is a part of a discursive context that embodies hegemonic relations, and a close study of the nature of questions and answers may provide concrete understanding of the interplay between domination and skewed "reciprocity." At the very least, the reader deserves a transcription of the inquisition register itself to be in a better position to test the use and the interpretation made of it. When a source such as this is used simply as a quarry or as an occasional reference point for a story or an analytic reduction, it is effectively silenced, and the reader is at a loss in trying to come to a critical appreciation of the historian's account. This difficulty is especially pronounced in *The Cheese and the Worms,* where it is often impossible to address critically the question of what is coming from Menocchio and what is being projected by Ginzburg. At points in any interpretation, it may be impossible to answer this kind of question, but one needs some basis for raising it and for estimating when it may become undecidable, especially when the interpretative component of the account is marked and the transferential relation between the historian and his subject is particularly intense. It is in making public the texts one interprets and in providing a close, critical, and self-critical reading of them that social history may acquire something of value from procedures that are (or should be) important in intellectual history. To make these points is not to rule out the task of employing documents in the inferential reconstruction of other events and processes; it is, however, to add another layer of inquiry to that task—one that may render it more cognitively responsible.

I have brought together scattered remarks in *The Cheese and the Worms* to form a configuration of ideas somewhat different from the one uppermost in Ginzburg's argument. My emphasis would be on the complex, often distorted interaction of levels or aspects of culture and the attendant relation between orthodoxy and heterodoxy in social and intellectual life. Oral popular culture, of which peasant culture is a component, can be reconstituted only in a very tentative way, given the nature of the evidence. And forces of resistance to hegemonic culture are, as Ginzburg indicates, often among the silences of the past for which the historian must attempt to account. But this attempt does not imply that the historian's "voice" fully masters the past. Nor does it exclude the necessity of investigating modes of accommodation to dominant forces, for these provide a realistic context for appreciating the more or less exceptional or widespread nature of resistance itself. Indeed the historian must be alert to the possibility of tensions and contradictions within as well as between levels of culture, including popular culture. Ginzburg criticizes the history of mentalities for its "insistence on the inert, obscure, unconscious elements in a given world view" and for "its decidedly classless character" (p. xxiii). But not only does he threaten to replicate on another level its insistence on a structural unconscious; he also tends to displace its assumption of cultural unity from society as a whole to relations within a class or a level of culture.

Hegemonic culture itself is not a homogeneous whole; it varies over time, and the very fissures or uncertainties in it at any given time may provide spaces in which resistance can manifest itself. In certain periods, it may even be difficult to discern what is hegemonic or orthodox. The Reformation and the Counter-Reformation did through conflict heighten unity within opposed groups, and there may have been "an increasingly rigid distinction between the culture of the dominant classes and artisan and peasant cultures" (p. 126). But the sixteenth century in general was a time when hegemony itself was at issue, and lines of communication were not entirely broken, notably (as Ginzburg notes) between segments of popular and high culture. The pre-Reformation Church could afford to be relatively tolerant insofar as challenges to it were not crystallized in large-scale, organized movements and alternative institutions. With the coming of the Reformation, the crust was not simply broken in ways that allowed heterodoxies to emerge. As in the first centuries of Christianity, the very nature of orthodoxy had to be defined (or redefined), and the scope of the challenges both from Protestants of various confessions and from more or less non-Christian heterodoxies (as well as from diverse amalgams) helped generate anxiety and dogmatic intolerance. The Catholic Church itself displayed some of the more spiritually "rigorous" traits of its Reformed critics—including their "seriousness" and anticarnivalesque impetus—not simply to do more effective battle with them but also because of the internally persuasive features of the newer ways. There is a significant exchange between Menocchio and the inquisitor in this respect. In answer to one of the recurrent questions concerning his discussions with others about articles of faith, Menocchio responds that he had spoken "jokingly with some about the articles of the faith." The inquisitor counters: "How is it that you were joking about matters of the faith? Is it proper to joke about the faith?" (quoted, p. 104). From a different, in certain respects an older, perspective, what is unfortunate is that these questions could be reduced to the fatuous level of rhetorical indignation. Yet, as Ginzburg indicates, the inquisitors themselves might at certain junctures be uncertain about belief or procedure, and this uncertainty allowed at least a little room for Menocchio's initiatives.

If there were more truly reciprocal relations among levels of culture that seem to have continued throughout the sixteenth century, they took place between segments of popular and high culture. Here, moreover, dominant and high culture cannot simply be equated. In one obvious sense, dominant or hegemonic culture may be seen as a form of high culture. And aspects of high culture (in the sense of works of a cultural elite) may reinforce hegemonic culture. But high culture may itself harbor forces of resistance and criticism that are most effective socially when they connect with aspects of popular culture. If Frances Yates is right, heterodox tendencies were at times quite prevalent, perhaps even "dominant," in cultural elites in the course of the sixteenth century.[6] And, as Ginzburg himself repeatedly notes, there were at least convergences between Menocchio's views and those advanced in the most "progressive" circles of high culture, particularly among humanistic "heretics."

At this point, one may return to the complex figure of Menocchio and the question of what that figure may tell us about the interaction of levels or aspects of culture at his time and over time. In his preface to the Italian edition, Ginzburg asserts that "even a limited case (and Menocchio certainly is this) can be representa-

6. See *Giordano Bruno and the Hermetic Tradition* (Chicago, 1964) and *The Occult Philosophy in the Elizabethan Age* (London, 1979).

tive" (p. xxi). But in what precise sense is he the representative bearer or exemplar of oral, popular, peasant culture? In some sense—but how precise about it can one be?—Menocchio is "representative." But he is also other than representative. He is exceptional, not a " 'typical' peasant" (p. xx)—not even (if you will excuse an atrocious pun) a run-of-the-mill miller. He seems exceptional in the way he articulates common beliefs and exceptional in his resistance to pressures both in his village community and in his inquisitorial trials. He is perhaps even exceptional in his own variant of metaphysical desire, in his "uncontrollable yearning 'to seek exalted things' "—a yearning that "tormented him" (p. 110). Even as an isolated old man beset with bitter irony, he was not entirely broken. This too seems rather exceptional.

But even in a more obviously sociocultural sense, there is something exceptional ("individual" might be a better word) about Menocchio, and this status—largely repressed throughout Ginzburg's text—seems to emerge forcefully in the concluding pages. I would suggest that Menocchio was "representative" and "exceptional" in the peculiar sense of being a liminal figure—a position that suited him for the role of scapegoat before the inquisition. His position was liminal between popular and elite as well as between oral and written culture. The idea that oral culture was Menocchio's primary grid seems particularly suspect in light of the way Menocchio was divided between the "world" of oral culture and that of the books that meant so much to him. Indeed the case of the other miller (Pighino) who was tried by the inquisition—a case Ginzburg introduces in good part to underwrite Menocchio's "representativeness"—also serves to stress his liminality. Pighino, while in certain ways a less impressive figure than Menocchio, may actually have attended readings of the famous heretic Paolo Ricci, better known as Camillo Renato (and also going by the humanistic name of Lisia Fileno). (See page 122.) Here there would be an actual discursive context linking segments of popular culture with heterodox segments of high culture. Even more strikingly, Ginzburg notes that Menocchio's trial in 1599 almost coincided with that of Giordano Bruno—a near coincidence that "seems to symbolize the twofold battle being fought against both high and low in this period of the Catholic hierarchy" (p. 127).

Yet Menocchio is also in certain respects situated at the threshold between popular and dominant culture. He very much wanted to enter into an exchange with the "higher-ups" and at times this desire fueled his impudence. In Ginzburg's words, Menocchio "felt the need to acquire the inherited knowledge of his adversaries, the inquisitors. In the case of Menocchio, in short, we perceive a free and aggressive spirit intent on squaring things with the culture of the dominant classes" (p. 118). This need, I would add, seems very modern, for it is one that confronts critics today on all levels of culture.

The complexity of this figure of resistance does not, however, stop here. Menocchio was in fact someone who had many social roles on the level of popular culture itself, prominently including those of peasant and miller. He tilled the land yet he dressed in the traditional white garb of the miller. Toward the end of his book, Ginzburg introduces considerations that indicate both the existence of certain tensions in the popular classes and the special status of millers in popular culture:

> The age-old hostility between peasants and millers had solidified an image of the miller—shrewd, thieving, cheating, destined by definition for the fires of hell. . . . The charge of heresy was wholly consistent with a stereotype such as this. Contributing to it was the fact that the mill was a place of meeting, of social relations, in a world that was predominantly closed and static. Like the inn and the shop it was a place for the exchange of ideas. . . . Their working conditions made millers—like innkeepers, tavern keepers, and itinerant artisans—an occupational group especially receptive to new ideas and inclined to propagate them. Moreover, mills, generally located on the peripheries of settled areas and far from prying eyes, were well suited to shelter clandestine gatherings. (pp. 119–20)

So we have Menocchio—miller, peasant, and guitar player at feasts—resisting hegemonic culture yet wanting to engage it in controversy, having a deep interest in certain books, and transmitting oral culture that is linked to certain heterodox aspects of high culture. Could he also be called a proto-intellectual, an early version of what Gramsci was to call the "organic" intellectual, one coming from the popular classes yet able to engage hegemonic and high culture in the interest of the oppressed? Perhaps. Ginzburg indicates how Menocchio confronted a problem that has become familiar in the modern period: that of addressing a split audience. "He presented a simplified, exoteric view of his ideas to the ignorant villagers: 'If I could speak I would, but I do not want to speak.' The more complex, esoteric view, instead, was reserved for the religious and secular authorities whom he so eagerly wished to approach: 'I said,' he informed his judges at Portogruaro, 'that if I had permission to go before the pope, or a king, or a prince who would listen to me, I would have a lot of things to say; and if he had me killed afterwards, I would not care.'" (pp. 65–66)

Whatever may have been the case in Menocchio's time, later periods were to manifest exacerbated forms of this problem, and intellectuals might turn away from the need to speak in two voices, as popular culture itself seemed beleaguered if not effaced, and newer modes of cultural dominance took shape. Even the appropriation of older popular traditions in high culture might take esoteric or hermetic forms that made them inaccessible to a wider audience. And, as Ginzburg remarks in a footnote, the modern period added another dimension of culture, mass or commodified culture—something that did not yet exist in the sixteenth century, at least in anything approximating its modern form (p. 130n). Commodified culture affects all other levels of culture and has complex relations to hegemonic culture in general and official state culture in particular. The extent to which it has assimilated popular culture itself as well as the extent to which it is punctuated by forces of criticism and resistance is an intricate story whose recounting would take us too far afield.

Still, Menocchio's proximity to us, "a man like ourselves, one of us," a man whose story "implicitly poses a series of questions for our own culture and for us" (p. xii), is a many-sided issue. What I would stress in conclusion is the bearing of the transferential dimension of research on the historical profession itself. In academics we have, in our own small way, witnessed the emergence of various heterodoxies, and we are at a point where the very definition of orthodoxy is in question. As always, there is a significant relation between intellectual and institutional matters. To see Menocchio predominantly as the bearer of an oral, popular culture that is given a privileged status in interpretation easily functions to reinforce hegemonic relations in professional historiography. If a certain level of culture represents primordial reality, then it is a very short step to the assumption that those who study it are the "real" historians, those who focus on the most important things. One could easily gather oral and written evidence to support the contention that a number of historians have taken this step. The result is a bizarre and vicious paradox whereby a vicarious relation to the oppressed of the past serves as a pretext for contemporary pretensions to dominance. A different understanding of problems may further a more accurate account of the interaction among aspects of culture in the past as well as a constructive conception of their desirable relations in the present, both within the historical profession and beyond it.[7]

7. Praise for *The Cheese and the Worms* has been high, but the reception of the book among specialists has not been devoid of critical response. For the most extensive critical analysis of it, which in limited ways converges with the argument in this essay, see Paola Zambelli, "Uno, due, tre, mille Menocchio?" *Archivo storico italiano* 137 (1979): 51–90. This is the critique to which Ginzburg tries to reply in the long footnote to the English edition (pp. 154–55) which I have discussed. See also the reservations in the reviews of Samuel Cohn Jr., *Journal of Interdisciplinary History* 12 (1982): 523–25; Erik H. C. Midelfort, *Catholic Historical Review* 68 (1982): 513–14; and Valerio Valeri, *Journal of Modern History* 54 (1982): 139–43. Although it appeared before the publication of *The Cheese and the Worms*, Anne Jacobson Schutte's "Carlo Ginzburg" (*Journal of Modern History* 48 [1976]: 296–315) contains some observations that are pertinent to its argument. Schutte stresses the role of Ginzburg's obvious animus against the Catholic Church and in favor of "pagan" culture. I have chosen to emphasize the somewhat less apparent bearing of Ginzburg's approach upon the historical profession itself. Schutte also raises some probing questions about the limitations of Ginzburg's use of inquisition registers as sources.

3

Is Everyone a *Mentalité* Case? Transference and the "Culture" Concept

> There is at least one spot in every dream at which it is
> unplumbable—a navel, as it were, that is its point of
> contact with the unknown. . . . This is the dream's navel,
> the spot [or place: *Stelle*] where it reaches down into [or
> straddles: *aufsitzt*—with no implication that it touches
> bottom] the unknown. The dream-thoughts to which we
> are led by interpretation cannot, from the nature of
> things, have any definite endings [or are interminable:
> *ohne Abschluss*]; they are bound to branch out in every
> direction into the intricate network [or netlike
> entanglement: *netzartige Verstrickung*—with a stronger
> connotation that one may lose one's way in its trap-like
> folds] of our world of thought. It is at some point where
> this meshwork is particularly close that the dream-wish
> grows up, like a mushroom out of its mycelium.
>
> SIGMUND FREUD, *The Interpretation of Dreams*

THE elusive ideal of a consensus in society sought by an earlier
generation of historians seems to have been displaced onto the
community of historians themselves, for the concept of "culture"
is well on the way to becoming the totem for a consensus on the
proper object and method of research in historiography. The con-

cept has already won its privileged place in anthropology, and it is from that discipline that recent historians have made the greatest borrowings in their attempt to define and apply the "culture" concept. Yet the very proliferation of definitions is a sign of the impediments to consensus and of the need for inquiry into the problems left unresolved by an almost oneiric reliance on the concept of culture, especially when it is used to effect an uncritical assimilation of intellectual and social history.

One such problem is the transferential relation between practices in the past and historical accounts of them. I use "transference" in the modified psychoanalytic sense of a repetition-displacement of the past into the present as it necessarily bears on the future. "Transference" is bound up with a notion of time not as simple continuity or discontinuity but as repetition with variation or change—at times traumatically disruptive change. Transference causes fear of possession by the past and loss of control over both it and oneself. It simultaneously brings the temptation to assert full control over the "object" of study through ideologically suspect procedures that may be related to the phenomenon Freud discussed as "narcissism."

Narcissism is a one-sided but alluring response to the anxiety of transference. It involves the impossible, imaginary attempt totally to integrate the self; it is active in the speculative effort to elaborate a fully unified perspective, and its self-regarding "purity" entails the exorcistic scapegoating of the "other" that is always to some extent within. As Freud indicated, the desirable but elusive objective of an exchange with an "other" is to work through transferential displacement in a manner that does not blindly replicate debilitating aspects of the past. Transference implies that the considerations at issue in the object of study are always repeated with variations—or find their displaced analogues—in one's account of it, and transference is as much denied by an assertion of the total difference of the past as by its total identification with one's own "self" or "culture."

The difficulty is to develop an exchange with the "other" that is both sensitive to transferential displacement and open to the challenge of the other's "voice." In this sense, it is a useful critical fiction to believe that the texts or phenomena to be interpreted may answer one back and even be convincing enough to lead one to change one's mind. Historians' relation to an "object" of study is, however, invariably mediated by the words (and silences) of those they deem to be significant interlocutors, and a beneficial effect of the anxiety of transference may be to provoke historians to ask whether questions raised in bordering areas or disciplines are relevant to their own research.

At present, historians are quite willing to listen to neighbors in the social sciences, but the less manageable contributions of literary critics and philosophers are often met with extreme suspicion if not active resistance. Yet transference may be blindest when disciplinary or subdisciplinary boundaries and protocols of research become the foundations for a self-enclosed frame of reference that induces the methodological scapegoating—the exclusion or reduction—of phenomena and perspectives that cannot be fully adjusted to it. The problem of transference in all its dimensions arises in an especially pointed way, I think, in the relation of intellectual and sociocultural historians to one another as well as to their "objects" of study.

A transferential relation is especially difficult to negotiate critically in view of the complexity of "culture" in the modern period and the challenge of elaborating concepts to investigate it. With reference to modern Western (particularly Western European) countries, one must at the very least distinguish among various aspects or levels of culture that require further differentiations within each category: high or elite culture, popular culture, and mass culture. What are these aspects or levels of culture? What are some important ways in which they interact, or fail to interact, at any given time and over time? What are some further differentiations within these aspects or levels? How do they—indeed do they—add up to a more or less unified conception of general or common culture? And how have intellectual and sociocultural history often replicated or "transferred" the problems besetting their "objects" of study in their own disciplinary protocols and procedures?

High or elite culture generally refers to the artifacts of cultural elites in the arts and sciences—novels, poems, paintings, philosophical treatises, scientific discoveries, and so forth. In a larger sense, it may also refer to the culture (or discursive practice) within which artifacts appear—literary culture in contrast to scientific culture, for example. High or elite culture has of course been characterized by pronounced differentiation or even fragmentation in the modern period, giving rise to difficulties of communication between various elites as well as between elites and untutored or non-expert "lay" segments of the population.

High or elite culture may also refer to the culture of other elites—political, socioeconomic, military, bureaucratic, academic, and so forth. The cultures of these elites have problematic relations to one another and to elite culture in the first sense. For example, Europe, in some degree of significant contrast with the United States, has had social elites who held cultural elites and their artifacts in high regard (at least as "symbolic capital") and thus conferred social prestige on artists and intellectuals. But a typical phenomenon in modern culture has been the "alienation" of cultural elites from other elites and from the dominant sociocultural context with its "philistinism" and institutionalized or patterned forms of "social pathology," "internal contradiction," and misguided values. Modern intellectuals in quest of critical distance and alternatives have looked both to (real or fictionalized) aristocratic values and to oppressed groups and cultures or have faced severe crisis, especially when the isolation of their group was intensified by personal isolation. Indeed, as a dangerous supplement offering society ambivalent gifts, intellectuals have often found themselves in—and at times have actively cultivated—the role of scapegoat.

A related issue is the status of official culture in the sense of culture actively supported by the state. Opera, for example, was an object of disproportionate funding by certain governments in the nineteenth century, and officially sponsored academies of painting posed obstacles to innovation in art.[1] The role of government funding in the twentieth century has been particularly significant in the natural sciences, but it has also affected other areas, and the policies that inform it are often compatible with those of private funding agencies. Indeed the decisive private/public dichotomy, its permutations over time, and its tendency to become both blurred and transparently ideological with the rise of state intervention, big business, and big labor, have been prominent forces affecting all levels of culture in the modern period. Debates over what belongs in the private or public "sphere"—and whether this massive binary opposition is itself one of the most mystifying ideologies in history—have been among the most agitated and momentous in intellectual life. The very notion of a "public sphere," as in the work of Jürgen Habermas, has itself been related to an understanding of political culture that goes beyond the bounds of official culture or the institutions of the state. It encompasses the area in which private citizens address political issues that always touch upon the organization and policies of the state, but that may do so in the form of criticism or even of attempts to rehabilitate an older notion of the *polis* or the *res publica;* or, indeed, to rearticulate the very nature of political life. One contested issue has been the extent to which various groups in society have participated actively in the public sphere and displayed a viable political culture or, by contrast, the extent to which they have been excluded by hegemonic forces or depoliticized and, in a sense, "bought off" by compensatory mechanisms in a commodity system and a consumer society.[2]

1. There is a good discussion of official culture in Arno Mayer, *The Persistence of the Old Regime* (New York, 1981). Mayer's treatment of high culture (notably the work of Nietzsche) displays many of the tendencies I discuss later in this essay.

2. On this issue, see the works of Jürgen Habermas, especially *Strukturwandel der Öffentlichkeit* (Neuwied and Berlin, 1965). See also Peter Uwe Hohendahl, *The Institution of Criticism* (Ithaca, 1982).

Popular culture often refers to the culture of specific groups, especially peasants and workers. It typically encompasses such phenomena as popular religion, witchcraft, and folklore. But it also includes the culture of work and its relation to the culture of play (notably the carnivalesque) in "popular" groups. Here one issue is the role of artisanal activity and values in relation to the disruptive forces of outwork and factory labor, as well as the rise of newer working-class elites (such as highly skilled machine-tool specialists) in the factory setting itself. Artisanal work was embedded in a specific culture with its organization of trade, its work rhythms, and its corporative institutions and practices. It also came accompanied by hierarchical differences as well as paternalistic relations in the workshop and forms of solidarity and sectarianism within and between trades. How this culture of work interacted with—and was transformed by—newer processes of industrial capitalism with its competitive values and work ethic is a sociologically and regionally differentiated story that is just beginning to unfold in all its complexity.[3]

Older rhythms of work were articulated with rhythms of play, and the disruption and transformation of the one involved the disruption and transformation of the other. Carnival and the culture of the carnivalesque in general (ribald humor, charivari, grotesquerie, parody, irony, etc.) were opposed by religious and secular powers for a variety of reasons: their incompatibility with reformed religion; their possible role in political protest; their infringement of a methodical work ethic; their manifest clash with utilitarian values; their indulgence of behavior that seemed too brutish or brutal in the context of more "enlightened" values. Given active opposition to them on many fronts and for heterogeneous reasons, carnivalesque phenomena tended to decline or to be integrated in more one-dimensional and domesticated form, notably by the state (parades, pageants) and the family (the domes-

3. See, for example, William Sewell, *Work and Revolution in France* (Cambridge, England, 1980) and E. P. Thompson, *The Making of the English Working Class* (New York, 1963).

tic celebration of holidays, the situation comedies of daily life). In muted but still potent ways, older carnivalesque practices were taken up in (or translated into) high cultural artifacts and at times used to protest newer sociocultural developments. But even in artists and writers who strained to make contact with "popular" groups, the adaptation of older modes might assume sophisticated or erudite forms that made them inaccessible to a larger audience. This tendency was carried to an extreme in art that, both impudently and defensively, turned its back on society to affirm its own autonomy, experimentalism, or the value of "art for art's sake." Most important perhaps, the rise of mass culture threatened to "co-opt" both popular and elite forms by converting "leisure time" into the space for the consumption of culture as a commodity. The translation of culture into the commodity form also posed the more general problem of the sale of all activities on the market, a phenomenon crucial to Marx's indictment of wage labor as prostitution and to Flaubert's image of the prostitution of everything (except unvarnished prostitution) in modern culture. The often paradoxical task of critics was to contrive a way to counter the "co-optation" of criticism and carnivalization themselves.[4]

Before turning to mass culture and the appropriately uglysounding process of "commodification," I would note that popular culture is sometimes used in a second sense, that of general or common culture. What this usage easily obscures is the extent to which hegemony is the mystifying reality behind the false face of unity or generality. Here the issue is that of the differential participation of various groups in hegemonic culture and the different functions and interests such culture serves. One question is the extent to which hegemonic culture is unified and the extent to

4. The works of Mikhail Bakhtin have inspired the research of historians inquiring into the problems raised in this paragraph. See, for example, Natalie Z. Davis, *Society and Culture in Early Modern France* (Stanford, 1975). See also my "Bakhtin, Marxism, and the Carnivalesque" in *Rethinking Intellectual History* (Ithaca, 1983) and my attempt to discuss the relation of Flaubert to the carnivalesque in *"Madame Bovary" on Trial* (Ithaca, 1982).

which it is itself marked by tensions and even contradictions between and within dominant groups or institutions (factions of the aristocracy; aristocracy and bourgeoisie; older and newer bourgeoisie; political, bureaucratic, social, military, economic, and academic elites, and so forth). It is both intellectually and politically reductive to rely on an excessively "hegemonic" conception of hegemony, e.g., either in terms of a "conquering bourgeoisie" or in terms of "the persistence of the old regime." Such a conception may obscure the manner in which fissures in the dominant "system" create areas in which resistance can manifest itself and create difficulties for hegemonic forces. A related question is how subordinate groups or classes assimilate hegemonic culture and how their own culture and values may in turn be affected or assimilated by it. The response of oppressed groups to hegemonic culture may range from active resistance to more or less forced "adaptation," and this response is further complicated by the relation of oppressed groups to one another. Indeed hegemonic culture that is resisted in certain ways may be accepted in others, often with a blindness to the resultant contradiction. A divided response to hegemonic practices that replicates forms of domination within oppressed groups or their advocates is particularly significant with respect to the problem of class and gender. Opposition to the existing class structure may be accompanied by the tendency to ignore the issue of sexism or to see it as a mere adjunct of economic exploitation. Yet what has become increasingly evident in the recent past is the manner in which the intricate relation between class and gender must be a crucial concern for a critical historiography.

Mass culture refers to the conversion of culture into a commodity that is produced and distributed in accordance with the principles of other economic sectors. With commodification, the opposition between work and play collapses at a crucial juncture, for play as leisure time is itself recycled into a market system. (Indeed leisure time might be defined as commodified play.) At the same time, however, work and play are effectively split off or "alienated" from each other, with work being defined predominantly in terms of instrumental or even technical efficiency and play being confined to a separate sphere of leisure-time activity. In this sense, leisure is divorced from production, but it is recaptured as consumption and serviced by units of production or "culture industries" specializing in the satisfaction of leisure-time needs. While the extent and implications of the commodification of culture are major problems in modern history, it would be self-defeating to indulge an indiscriminate attack on the "one-dimensionality" of mass culture and to ignore countercurrents or forces of resistance in it and in dimensions of elite and popular culture. It would be equally self-defeating simply to convert literary criticism and intellectual history into negatively critical sociologies of the "culture industry," for this would help extirpate modes of interpretation sensitive to countercurrents both in the artifacts of the past and in one's own discourse about them.

An obvious problem for a critical historiography is how to address the relations among high, popular, and mass culture in a fashion that allows for a mutually informative and challenging interaction between various perspectives and subdisciplines. Social and intellectual historians have not been altogether successful in achieving such an interaction, in good part because those turning to "culture" as a unifying concept have been insufficiently sensitive to the complex intellectual and ideological issues covered, and sometimes obscured, by its use.

Intellectual history has traditionally concentrated on elite culture, in the sense of the artifacts of cultural elites, often in splendid isolation from all the other problems I have mentioned. It has often considered all culture below the level of a narrow elite stratum to be the irredeemable realm of degraded simulacra not worthy of sustained attention. It has thereby obscured the conventional or symptomatic aspects of elite culture as well as the very problem of the variable nature and possibilities of its interaction with other aspects or levels of culture. Thus it has tended to replicate some of the most extreme and dubious sides of elite

culture itself—its snobbish exclusiveness, self-enclosure, formalism, and hegemonic pretensions. And it has frequently done so
in abstraction from the countercurrents that do exist in elite
culture itself. Here one has the sterile paradox of canonization of
the "greats": the artifacts of high culture may in the process of
canonization be interpreted in ways that avoid their contestatory
and unsettling sides, and their exceptional qualities may be distorted into an unqualified idea of their quasi-religious, transcendent, or "sublime" status. Indeed the history-of-ideas approach
typically relied on idealist philosophical premises, and it frequently
reduced the artifacts of high culture to documents of a detached
"mind," "symbolic form," or "unit-idea."

Contemporary sociocultural history was in part motivated by a
justifiable revolt against an abstracted history of ideas. But it has
often tended simply to reverse the latter's assumptions (through
reductionism) and to replicate its documentary treatment of artifacts (as symptoms of society or economy rather than mind). It
has also replicated an all-too-prevalent social reaction to intellectual history's objects of study (both artifacts and artists or intellectuals). For it has responded to the anxiety of transference through
processes of reduction or exclusion that amount to at least methodological scapegoating if not anti-intellectualism, and it has
thereby tended to deny the contestatory dimensions of high culture
and the challenge of forging new links between it and popular
culture—a challenge that confronts historians themselves in the
very language they use to interpret aspects of culture. Sociocultural
history has sometimes proceeded under the banner of a populism
("history from the bottom up") that has become less political and
increasingly methodological, taking social research in directions
that are of little significance or even diversionary both for the
oppressed in society and for those attempting to develop a critical
historiography. In any event, its populism often repeats rather
blindly the scapegoating propensities of populism in society. The
result is prepossessing and intimidating when social history claims
to be a "total history" or at least the cynosure to which all other
historical approaches must be referred.

Social history has recently risen to a position of prominence if not of hegemony in the historical profession, and its important sociocultural variant has led to a redefinition of intellectual history as a social history of ideas or *mentalités.* It is alarming that the uncritical characteristics I have specified at times appear in the very best work done in sociocultural and related forms of intellectual history—not merely in their average or inferior products. In accordance with the principle that one should address criticism to the strongest rather than the weakest exemplifications of a tendency one questions, I would like to support my admittedly harsh assertions by examining the work of two justly renowned and influential historians, Carl Schorske and Robert Darnton. The limited nature of my inquiry into their valuable contributions must be kept in mind. Indeed the contagious effects of the scapegoat mechanism are notorious, and I would fall blindly into the dubious kind of transferential relation I am criticizing if I claimed to be doing full justice to their work or even eliciting its incontestably dominant features. But I think that the characteristics I shall discuss are operative to a sufficiently troubling degree, and I shall try to indicate currents in the work of Schorske and Darnton that themselves provide some basis for placing these characteristics in question.

Schorske's work focuses on high culture. While he does provide some discussion of popular and mass culture, his more insistent aim is to connect high culture with political culture and the role of other elites in society. His very understanding of the high culture of fin-de-siècle Vienna is in terms of its status as a response to the modern crisis of liberal political culture. He contends that the Viennese cultural elite was first alienated, together with its middle-class audience, before it became alienated from society as a whole, and the form its alienation took was a turn away from politics itself toward aesthetic and psychological escapism.[5]

Schorske clearly recognizes the limitations of both an ahistorical, internalist formalism that remains fixated on syn-

5. *Fin-de-Siècle Vienna: Politics and Culture* (New York, 1980).

chronic analysis and a reductive contextual historicism that converts all artifacts into mere representative documents. "Historians
had been too long content to use the artifacts of high culture as
mere illustrative reflections of political or social developments, or
to relativize them to ideology."[6] Yet instead of trying to rethink the
entire relation between artifact or text and context in a way that
contests both formalistic and historicist methods, Schorske opts
for a *combination* of the two with an explicit emphasis upon the
conventional historicist desire for the big picture or the panoramic
"larger context." Abjuring "the aim of the humanistic textual
analyst" directed toward "the greatest possible illumination of a
cultural product," the historian for Schorske will "spin yarn ser-
viceable enough for the kind of bold patterned fabric he is called
upon to produce."[7] The historian thus becomes a weaver of sturdy
goods for everyday use in contrast to that *Hetaera esmeralda,* the
"humanistic textual analyst," who turns out trickier items that
seem to carry the connotative stamp of luxury or even superfluity.
Schorske's homespun analogy functions to keep the intellectual
and cultural historian in a craft whose products are immediately
recognized as respectable by other historians—products securely
distanced from the output of literary critics. One question that
nonetheless arises as Schorske carries out his program is whether
the unstable combination of guarded formalism and contextualist
historicism tends to collapse in a reductive direction whereby the
artifact or text is explained as a very restricted, indeed symptomatic response to a "larger context" construed in an altogether
particular manner.

   Schorske is quite frank in revealing why he was led to study fin-
de-siècle Vienna, and his motivation in research is in no sense
peculiar to him.

   Having encountered through teaching the baffling problem of
   finding some related characteristics for pluralized, post-

6. Ibid., p. xxi.
7. Ibid., pp. xxi–xxii.

Nietzschean culture, I had been made aware of the need to proceed piecemeal, recognizing the autonomous analytic modes necessary to understanding the several strands of cultural innovation. At the same time, the political and intellectual life of post-war America suggested the crisis of a liberal polity as a unifying context for simultaneous transformation in the separate branches of culture. The fact that Freud and his contemporaries aroused new interest in America in itself suggested Vienna as a unit of study. Finally, to keep history's synoptic potential intact when both the culture itself and the scholarly approaches to it were becoming de-historicized and pluralized, a well-circumscribed social entity, reasonably small but rich in cultural creativity was needed.[8]

Schorske was thus motivated by the familiar desire of historians to find order in seeming chaos, at least on a methodological level, by providing a coherent, synoptic account of incoherent, fragmented phenomena. Schorske obviously did not want to join in the "death dance of principles" that he beheld in Viennese high culture. But is his procedure itself ideological, insofar as it creates the impression of a possible methodological solution to substantive sociocultural problems? Might not the almost obsessive theme of a guilt-ridden escape from politics into the psyche and art both oversimplify the object of study and indicate unacknowledged tensions in the psychologizing historian of art? The historian seems to acquire a deceptive hold on problems through a methodological device: the topical choice of a city and the employment of manageably synoptic, indeed reductive, protocols of interpretation. How can such an approach enable one to come to terms with that bigger and less manageable world for which the hothouse Viennese microcosm was in some sense a "tryout"? Is that approach acceptable even for the little Viennese world?

The unifying theme of a crisis in liberal political culture seems doubtful on the basis of Schorske's own analysis of the situation. It is much more symptomatic both of the recurrent speculative desire

8. Ibid., p. xxv.

to achieve "narcissistic" closure and of Schorske's concerns in the United States of the 1950s than it is of fin-de-siècle Vienna. For Schorske himself provides abundant evidence that political liberalism in the Austro-Hungarian Empire was a relatively small and beleaguered force that came to power only during a brief and evanescent period at the end of the nineteenth century. The "crisis" of liberalism was at best a part of a much larger and more complex crisis—dynastic, national, international, ethnic, sexual, class—that can be centered on it only through a dubious tropological movement. To see that larger crisis in the primary, unified light of a crisis of a liberal polity may result in a largely fanta-sied Vienna. It is only in a more tentative, explicitly counterfactual fashion that one may argue that things might have gone better in Viennese high culture had a liberal polity and its preconditions been more in evidence at the time.

In addition, it is questionable whether the artifacts and texts Schorske discusses can themselves be unified by the attempt to envision them as various symptomatic, escapist responses even to the larger crisis. For these artifacts and texts have dimensions that may help to provide a critical perspective both on that crisis and on the recurrent problem of the desire for unity or consensus vis-à-vis the forces that contest it. This issue becomes especially insistent in Schorske's most extensive textual analysis—that of Freud's *Interpretation of Dreams*—for Schorske relies on a method of psychological reductionism that itself extracts one current from Freud's own texts but does not explicitly counter or problematize it with other currents that are quite active in those texts. Indeed in Schorske's own text, the quest for unity through a reductive psychologism superimposed on a reductive socioculturalism (artifacts as symptomatic responses to a crisis in liberal culture) itself confronts a paradoxical mirror image on a stylistic level. An almost Viennese flair for the elaborate elegance of a nicely turned phrase and a butterflylike delicacy in moving from *topos* to *topos* ("postholing," in Schorske's own deceptively down-to-earth metaphor) engender an enchanting world of words that at times seem as much to reflect off one another as to refer to Viennese "reality."

Schorske's interpretation of Freud may rely overmuch on a view prevalent in the 1950s, one given ironic voice in Philip Rieff's well-known study of Freud.[9] Here Freud becomes the discoverer of introspective, psychological man who turns away from the larger "realities" of politics and society to find sanctuary in the private psyche, its egocentric labyrinths and familial scenes. In the almost self-involved eloquence of the passage with which Schorske concludes his essay on Freud, he leaves the reader with this image of the old psychologist:

> The brilliant, lonely, painful discovery of psychoanalysis, which made it possible for Freud to overcome his Rome neurosis, to kneel at Minerva's ruined temple, and to regularize his academic status was a counterpolitical triumph of the first magnitude. By reducing his own political past and present to an epiphenomenal status in relation to the primal conflict between father and son, Freud gave his fellow liberals an a-historical theory of man and society that could make bearable a political world spun out of orbit and beyond control.[10]

This partially convincing portrait might be both further detailed by recent feminist critiques of Freud and made to apply transferentially to the quest for a unified method of sociocultural study in the context of contemporary America. It nonetheless obscures or denies the forces in Freud that radically challenge the idea that one may respond to political and social "realities" by an ahistorical, compensatory escape into the private self. Some of these forces were evoked in the passage from the *Interpretation of Dreams* that serves as my epigraph—a passage that addresses the very quest for a unified and self-unifying interpretative theory. But, in the more specific terms that Schorske himself touches on, who more than Freud taught us to suspect the escapism of a private, compensatory response to a public problem? One might even argue that Freud cleared one path for rethinking the problem of political culture by subtly extending the analysis of relations of power and authority

9. Philip Rieff, *Freud: The Mind of the Moralist* (New York, 1959).
10. *Fin-de-Siècle Vienna*, p. 203.

into the family setting, thereby broaching the issue of a politics of everyday life. To read Freud primarily as an escapist, frustrated liberal is to foreclose the possibly critical uses of psychoanalysis that were stressed by the Frankfurt school and to ignore the problem of the institutional implications of the more complex "Freud-on-Freud" readings developed by "post-structuralists." Such a reading also carries with it the tendency to replicate in one's own analysis the depoliticizing, scapegoating tendencies of the larger social forces that Schorske sincerely opposes. Finally, it is deceptive to reinforce one's case for Freud's escapism by suggesting that Freud might have become a politician like Victor Adler. The point is not so much that the path Freud took might be argued to have had more basic or at least longer-term political value. It is rather that comparisons of this sort are specious in that they envision as mutually exclusive options what are better interpreted as complementary approaches, even in a context that made "effective" political intervention for Jews a highly problematic issue in any event.[11]

11. It is instructive to compare Schorske's treatment of Freud with that to be found in such works as Herbert Marcuse, *Eros and Civilization* (Boston, 1955), Jürgen Habermas, *Knowledge and Human Interests* (Boston, 1971), and Gerard Radnitzky, *Contemporary Schools of Metascience* (Chicago, 1968), on the one hand, and Samuel Weber, *The Legend of Freud* (Minneapolis, 1982), Jean Laplanche, *Life and Death in Psychoanalysis* (Baltimore, 1976), and Geoffrey Hartman, ed., *Psychoanalysis and the Question of the Text* (Baltimore, 1978), on the other. One might argue that the larger problem is how to reconceptualize the relations between sociopolitical and psychoanalytic interpretation in terms quite different from those employed by Schorske. See also my "Marxism and Intellectual History" in *Rethinking Intellectual History* (Ithaca, 1983). One might further note that some of Schorske's other essays, especially the ones on Klimt and on Schoenberg and Kokoschka, do indicate how certain works were not simply escapist symptoms of the most negative aspects of society and culture but also significant embodiments of critical and adversarial response to them. Yet Schorske tends to make his own final interpretative gesture one that reveals the ultimately self-involved and superfluous nature of Viennese high culture, often at the cost of reinforcing the fatal split between art and life or even of obscuring traces of resistance to the tendencies he ostensibly deplores. It is difficult to tell whether the principal exception to this procedure is motivated by the belief, shared by orthodox Marxists, that art is irrelevant to "real" social change or by considerations that are primarily aesthetic, for Schorske concludes his book with the

Robert Darnton's focus is not high culture but the seemingly more popular levels on the cultural scale. In his project for a social history of ideas, he has often been perceived as a mediator of the methods of the *Annales* school in this country, especially in the light of its recent move toward the study of collective *mentalités*. His manifest objective is to illuminate the ideological origins and unfolding of the French Revolution, and he shifts attention from high Enlightenment *philosophes* to the role of relatively minor figures who were more widely read at their own time. In his own way, Darnton is also in quest of the elusive Grail of much historiography: managing complexity by projecting "order and perspicuity" (in Gibbon's phrase) on the historical record. He has unearthed a rich archive—that of the *Société Typographique de Neuchâtel*—and he draws from it enormous quantities of new information about the low Enlightenment world of dimmer luminaries. This reliance on a given source is itself a unifying factor in his recent research. But his more comprehensive device for synthesizing his material is to combine a selective reading of high culture with a more dismissive or exclusionary attitude toward it as "unrepresentative" of its time and of little causal importance in the flow of ordinary events.

Even those who tend to accept Darnton's particular version of the *Annales* message and identify with his mission nonetheless note his willingness to reduce the exceptional or the problematic to the unexceptional and readily categorized dimensions of a collective

---

conventional narrative device of pointing to an enigmatic ray of light at the end of an almost unbearably long and dark tunnel. As he tells the reader in a tortuous proleptic remark in the Foreword: "In an eruptive outburst against the aestheticism of the *fin de siècle,* Kokoschka and Schoenberg devised new languages in painting and music to proclaim the universality of suffering in transcendent negation of the professed values of their society. With the definition of modern man as one 'condemned to recreate his own universe,' twentieth-century Viennese culture had found its voice" (p. xxix). The second portrait of Hofmannsthal in the penultimate essay may be more hopeful than the one in the first essay, on which it plays a poignant variation, largely because this change seems necessitated by the concluding movement of the narrative.

discourse. I quote from a highly laudatory review of Darnton's *Literary Underground of the Old Regime* which appeared in *The American Historical Review*—a review in which criticism of Darnton (which even in muted tones is rather rare in published sources) comes in the echo-like, distanced form of a reference to another reviewer's voice: "As Norman Hampson observed in *The New York Review of Books* (October 7, 1982, pp. 43–44), Darnton may fit writers like Voltaire, Marat, and Mercier too neatly into defined social categories, and at times he substitutes what writers 'must have felt' for what they actually wrote. Reading books as a force for change, Darnton may have to exercise more patience than he seems willing with works that were not *chroniques scandaleuses.* . . ."[12]

At times the more decisive gesture in Darnton is to exclude in outright fashion what does not fit his model of research. Recently he has more insistently advocated the study of Grub Street literature—the "underground" that does not appear on the reading lists of literary critics who study canonized classics. Darnton never proves that his best-sellers reflect more than the somewhat philistine and resentful mentality of their Grub Street writers. He can tell us relatively little about the way what sold well was actually read and used. Often his inferences about the "general public" are derogatory—in fact at least as derogatory as those of the most elitist student of high culture:

> Beyond the court and below the summit of salon society, the "general public" lived on rumors; and the "general reader" saw politics as a kind of nonparticipant sport, involving villains and heroes but no issues—except perhaps a crude struggle between good and evil or France and Austria. He probably read *libelles* as his modern counterpart reads magazines or comic books, but he did not laugh them off; for the villains and heroes were real to him; they were fighting for control of France. Politics was living folklore. And so, after enjoying *La*

12. Raymond Birn in *The American Historical Review* 88 (1983): 687.

gazette noire's titillating account of venereal disease, buggery, cuckoldry, illegitimacy, and impotence in the upper ranks of French society, he may have been convinced and outraged by its description of Mme Du Barry, "passing directly from the brothel to the throne."[13]

The remarkably fictionalized nature of this account, which passes without catching its breath from the written page to the reader's archival recesses, is enough to give one pause. The attempt to compare a critical reading of texts to actual processes of reception might involve Darnton in problems of interpretation that he generally avoids—although one can perhaps predict that the extension of his methods into the study of the reception of literature "in greatest demand" will itself rely on narrowly empirical procedures that also skirt issues of critical interpretation.[14] What

13. *The Literary Underground of the Old Regime* (Cambridge, Mass., 1982), p. 204.

14. Narrowly empirical techniques do in fact mark Thomas Schleich's *Aufklärung und Revolution: Die Wirkungsgeschichte Gabriel Bonnot de Mablys in Frankreich, 1740–1914* (Stuttgart, 1981), although Schleich focuses on the reception of the works of a figure whose intellectual and cultural status is at least controversial. Reviewing this book, Lionel Gossman writes: "In the deliberate choice of texts that offer the minimum of resistance to the historian's disposing of them 'scientifically,' it is difficult to avoid recognizing something very similar to that illusory sense of superiority, of which Nietzsche accused another generation of historians, no less active and successful than the present one. The resolutely antielitist commitment to the (preferably second-rate) text-as-object may also bring with it a whiff of philistinism. Although it is a minor point, it is disturbing that in his concluding reflections Schleich follows Darnton in classing Chamfort with Cailhava, Cubières, Garat, Roucher, Suard, and Target as a writer of mediocre talent and no real accomplishments, interested primarily in 'making it' in the literary world of the High Enlightenment. I cannot speak about the others in this list, but I find it hard to believe that anyone who has read Chamfort could accept this summary judgment of a writer Schopenhauer and Nietzsche placed on a par with Montaigne, La Rochefoucauld, and Lichtenberg. No doubt Schleich did not think it was necessary to read Chamfort, but there is no evidence that he was much affected by his reading of Mably, who may indeed be as dull as the nineteenth-century conservatives said he was. Now what kind of history of ideas or of literature will be produced by those who elect not to encounter the ideas and texts of the past as living forces in the present? What view of ideas and of literature, what respect for them can they have or evoke in others? What has happened to

Darnton often provides is a description of incipient mass culture and the conversion of literature into a commodity. But he at times does so with an uncritically engaging verve that may replicate certain of the more dubious traits of his Grub Street writers, notably a patronizingly anti-intellectual populism and a socio-psychological reductionism. Darnton's delineation of the more narrowly materialistic and self-interested motivations of certain figures is a realistic reminder that even intellectuals do not live by ideas alone, but the tendency to focus on considerations worthy of the feuilleton threatens to make one lose sight of the genuinely contestatory features of the "literary underground" itself.

I would like to discuss briefly two specific passages in Darnton where the tendency toward methodological scapegoating is pronounced. The first provides his rationale for investigating the "business of Enlightenment" through the analysis of the publishing industry. "The history of literature tends inevitably to anachronism. Because each age reconstructs literary experience in its own terms and each historian tampers with the canon of classics, literature refuses to remain fixed within interpretive schemata. Like Walter Benjamin's library, it is a state of mind, which can always be unpacked and rearranged. Yet there is something unsatisfying about the notion of literary history as an endless reshuffling of great books."[15]

What the unsatisfying something might be remains unclear. In Benjamin, whose own critical intelligence was nurtured on a close reading of classics, the object of attack was the social function of canonization in a literary and academic establishment, and the

---

Michelet's democratic yet pious dream of resuscitating the past and 'making history's silences speak'? On the evidence of its productivity and large work force, the business of Enlightenment is prospering as never before, but how will the accountants judge it when they come to examine the books?" (*American Historical Review* 88 [1983]: 404). I would add: Can Gossman's be dismissed as the voice of the "humanistic textual analyst" that, through some bizarre anomaly, has intruded itself into the pages of the *American Historical Review?*

15. *The Literary Underground of the Old Regime*, p. 167.

larger target was the humanist's inclination to obliterate the way
the greatest works of civilization were also documents of barba-
rism. One does not find this sort of trenchancy in Darnton. The
reference to Benjamin seems little more than nominal. What is
noteworthy is the fact that the continual reinterpretation of
"great" texts with its "anachronistic" aspects that are bound up
with political investments is itself seen as little more than a process
of "endless reshuffling." What perspective informs the reduction
of interpretation over time to endless reshuffling?

A second passage comes from one of Darnton's early seminal
articles. It displaces the exclusionary scapegoating of high culture
onto those intellectual historians for whom the interpretation of
texts, with the argument and revision of understanding it entails, is
something other than "reshuffling."

> The social history of ideas must move out of its armchair phase
> and into the archives, tapping new sources and developing new
> methods. For how can it be written from within the confines of
> even a first-rate library? To pull some Voltaire from the shelf is
> not to come into contact with a representative slice of intellec-
> tual life from the eighteenth century, because . . . the literary
> culture of the Old Regime cannot be conceived exclusively in
> terms of its great books. . . . The finances, milieux, and read-
> ership of the philosophes can only be known by grubbing in the
> archives.[16]

Aspects of Darnton's argument in this passage have the disarm-
ing validity of common sense. Of course one cannot conceive the

16. "In Search of the Enlightenment: Recent Attempts to Create a Social
History of Ideas," *Journal of Modern History* 43 (1971): 132. I would further note
that Darnton's binary opposition between the armchair and the archives recalls the
tendentious contrast drawn by certain anthropologists between "armchair" the-
orizing and fieldwork. In anthropology, this contrast has often fostered a self-
mystified understanding of fieldwork as untouched by theory and in closest
proximity to "authentic" native experience—fieldwork as the virginally pure
"real thing." Here the metaphor of "grubbing" invites the sort of psychoanalytic
interpretation toward which I would prefer to maintain a "hands-off" policy.

literary culture of the Old Regime exclusively in terms of its great
books, and one will not learn much about the finances, milieux,
and readership of the *philosophes* from their published writings.
But less obvious are such issues as the general framework within
which matters of this sort should be addressed, the status of a
critical reading of "great books" in intellectual history, and the
implications of a focus on the "representative slice of intellectual
life." One difficulty is the way Darnton's emphases lend themselves to an archival fetishism that does not critically relativize
archival research to the nature of the question being asked, but
rather evaluates the significance of all research in terms of whether
it permits the discovery of hitherto unknown and unpublished
information. The stress on "grubbing in the archives" reinforces
the idea that only the reporting and analysis of (preferably new)
facts satisfy the conditions of strictly historical knowledge. The
revised interpretation or reading of already published materials,
including the texts of important writers and intellectuals, does not
make a significantly cognitive contribution to historiography, even
when it is situated in the context of an attempt to rethink the
relations of high, popular, and mass culture. It amounts to endless-
ly reshuffling books one pulls from the shelf, a somewhat gratuitous activity that is perhaps the province of our old friend "the
humanistic textual analyst."[17]

17. I am of course criticizing neither social history nor archival research but the
indiscriminate mystique of both which is bound up with hegemonic pretensions.
Here it may be noted that for Freud a fetish is a substitute for a lost object, and it is
related to the quest for full identity and narcissistic unity. The archive as fetish is a
literal substitute for the "reality" of the past which is "always already" lost for the
historian. When it is fetishized, the archive is more than the repository of traces of
the past which may be used in its inferential reconstruction. It is a stand-in for the
past that brings the mystified experience of the thing itself—an experience that is
always open to question when one deals with writing or other inscriptions.
Observe, for example, this evocation of the archival experience by Felix Gilbert: "I
still remember the start I received when at the beginning of my studies in the
Florentine Archivio I looked through a volume of documents and found a message
signed in big letters: Cesare of France, Duke of Romagna and Valence. I doubt that
before I saw this writing I had ever really believed that the man about whom
Burckhardt and Nietzsche had written had ever really existed." (Introduction,

More remarkable than the manifest content of this passage is the familiar scenario it enacts and the turns of phrase with which it conveys its *leçon de morale*. The reader is treated to a telling displacement of La Fontaine's fable about the ant and the locust. The archival sociocultural historian is a busy little ant that is not afraid to dirty its "hands" with real labor as it stores up real knowledge. The intellectual historian who does not emulate it is a relaxed parasite who does little more than dilettantish, after-dinner reading. I would not subscribe to the unqualified denigration of "unproductive" activity in which Darnton indulges. But for anyone—intellectual historian or not—who reads closely what he or she pulls from the shelf, the image evoked in Darnton's passage must seem strangely out of place.

At this concluding point, I would like to suggest a partial answer to the question posed in my title, and I cannot refrain from offering my own *leçon de morale*. Everyone is indeed a *mentalité* case, but not exactly in the same way. Certain artifacts are exceptional products of cultural activity, and it is ill-advised, even self-defeating, to deny their critical power or uncanny ability to play uncommon variations on commonplace themes. It would, however, be equally misleading to promote them to a detached, transcendent plane or to espouse an elitist aesthetics of genius. A careful and, in certain respects, noncanonical reading of canonical texts, open to their contestatory dimensions and alert to the problem of how to relate them to artifacts and issues excluded from established canons, is in no sense a full answer to the transferential problem in the study of culture; it is, however, a part of any acceptable answer. The larger issue, which is crucial for the articulation of disciplinary and social relations, is that of the actual and desirable interaction among aspects or levels of culture. The very difficulty of this issue should be enough to indicate the questionableness of over-

---

Felix Gilbert and Stephen R. Graubard, eds., *Historical Studies Today* [New York, 1972], p. xv.) Here of course the archival experience is reinforced by the authority of the signature.

simplified methodological "solutions" to it, particularly when the latter give rise to a markedly anti-intellectual intellectual history.[18]

18. Robert Darnton's *The Great Cat Massacre* (New York, 1984) appeared after the completion of this essay. In it Darnton makes an often successful attempt to address issues in a manner that escapes a number of criticisms I have put forth. He focuses on the interaction of popular and elite culture in coping with common problems, and he provides a remarkable range of insightful forays into the culture of the Old Regime. He is still concerned with representative or exemplary reactions, but he also notes the limitations of reductive approaches to cultural meaning and points out the role of the exceptional in popular culture itself. I would take issue with certain of his interpretations. For example, in "Readers Respond to Rousseau" Darnton reads *La nouvelle Héloïse* in terms of the most unproblematic construal of authorial intention and proceeds to identify the response of a wealthy bourgeois reader of the time as that of Rousseau's intended ideal reader. This reader's response to the text approximates Darnton's own, and the curious convergence belies Darnton's untroubled insistence on the alterity of the *mentalités* of the Old Regime. More generally, the oversimplified understanding of the "otherness" of the past obviates the need to confront the more complex problem of "transference" in one's relation to it. But I nonetheless think that Darnton in this book makes a series of significant overtures in the attempt to recast the social history of ideas, especially by stressing the importance of reading artifacts as complex texts.

4

Writing the History
of Criticism Now?

Il y a plus affaire à interpréter les interprétations qu'à
interpréter les choses.

[There is more to-do about interpreting interpretations
than about interpreting things.]

MONTAIGNE

I N this chapter I would like to turn from problems of historiography in general and of social history in particular to a different
but related concern: writing the history of criticism. But my chapter heading is intentionally ambiguous. It could refer to writing, at
the present time, the history of criticism. Or it could refer to
writing the history of the present condition or state of criticism—
an inquiry into how critics got where they are. This ambiguity may
be seen as necessary in that the two enterprises are intimately
bound up with each other, and both are pertinent to historians
who not only tolerate but affirm the value of the tense conjunction
of scholarship and criticism. Indeed the question mark in my
heading indicates that the present state of criticism may render
radically problematic the attempt to write something resembling a
conventional history of events or developments leading up to it.

What is the present "condition" of criticism that resists being
treated as a *telos* toward which earlier events unfold? Philip Lewis

has written with admirable precision of the present in terms of a "post-structuralist condition"—a state of intellectual disarray and a "conditionality" that (especially in the recent writings of Jean-François Lyotard and Jacques Derrida) holds out the promise of at least micropolitical intervention in a "struggle for positive values."[1] In a broader survey of the current critical scene, Jonathan Culler has remarked:

> If the observers and belligerents of recent critical debates could agree on anything, it would be that contemporary critical theory is confusing and confused. Once upon a time it might have been possible to think of criticism as a simple activity practiced with different emphases. The acrimony of recent debate suggests the contrary: the field of criticism is contentiously constituted by apparently incompatible activities. Even to attempt a list—structuralism, reader-response criticism, deconstruction, Marxist criticism, pluralism, feminist criticism, semiotics, psychoanalytic criticism, hermeneutics, antithetical criticism, *Rezeptionsästhetik* . . . —is to flirt with an unsettling glimpse of the infinite that Kant calls the "mathematical sublime."[2]

After briefer discussions of feminist and reader-response criticism, Culler "centers" his own account on Derrida and his American progeny, and he vividly shows that there is indeed life after deconstruction. But the ellipsis in the passage quoted above intimates that Culler's list of current tendencies may be extended perhaps not to infinity but at least far enough to engender a frustrated or an awestruck sense of the uncanny. One could, for example, add such university-based, putatively anti-domesticating spin-off groups as poststructural jansenists (insistent on the paradoxical purity of Derridean philosophy), stylistic *convulsion-*

1. Philip E. Lewis, "The Post-Structuralist Condition," *Diacritics* 12:1 (1982): 1–24.
2. Jonathan Culler, *On Deconstruction: Theory and Criticism after Structuralism* (Ithaca, 1982), p. 17.

naires, schizoanalysts, libido boosters, assorted gnostics, and Nietzschean flash-dancers. When one begins to enumerate the names of figures within each tendency who nonetheless have significantly different emphases, one's problem undergoes exponential complication. Furthermore, not only the guides to thought but the very objects of criticism stray outside the realm of what have ordinarily been taken to be the proper topics of literary criticism. So-called literary critics today may be seen discussing Hegel, Saussure, John Austin, Wittgenstein, or Freud as readily as Homer, Shakespeare, Jane Austen, Wordsworth, or Faulkner. They may even show a marked preference for writers who are among the least readily classifiable. The canon, to the extent that there still is one, speaks in many alien tongues.

Two points would seem both apparent and significant. First, criticism no longer means, if it ever simply did, *sui generis* literary criticism. The discourses of criticism extend beneath and beyond the literary to intersect with philosophy, linguistics, the "human sciences," social criticism, and much else besides. Certain critical practices such as feminism and Marxism resist being classified as one tendency among others and at least claim to be an essential dimension of all valid criticism. One may even argue that criticism itself has no secure status as a metalanguage, for it repeats on its own level the problems and the possibilities of literature itself—a transferential relation that brings both the thrill of creative artistry and the agony of mastery uncrowned. Literary criticism seems little more than the designation for the arena where the agon or contest among various discursive practices has been particularly intense in the recent past. Whether this situation enables one to name a new genre called "criticism" or whether it contests generic classifications may be undecidable. In any event, what becomes pressing is the issue of the relation of "criticism" to established disciplines and to the possibility of newer institutional arrangements that would allow closer working relations among "critics."

A second point complicates the picture of contemporary criticism even more. The various discourses do not simply characterize discrete interpretative communities who, like the putative *Natur-völker* of an idealized yesteryear, enjoy an authoritative internal consensus that makes communication across group lines either impossible or a gratuitous expression of idle curiosity. The contemporary scene reveals, if you will permit the jargon, a high degree of internal alterity and dialogization. Any given interpretative community harbors a number of significant inner differences. A Hegelian Marxist, in accordance with a principle well known in political life, may feel more hostile toward a structural or a deconstructive Marxist than toward a neo-Aristotelian or a reader-response critic. A reader-response critic may appeal alternately to the actual, possible, plausible, uncanny, desirable, naive, necessary, or essential reader, and in each case he or she may invoke various critical strategies in addressing issues. A reader-response critic may even join contemporary exponents of positivism, notably those in social history and social psychology, by restricting research to empirically documented instances of how texts were—to parody Ranke—*eigentlich gelesen.* Or, more obliquely, he or she may shirk responsibility for argument and interpretation in research by displacing the critic's role onto a putative ideal reader or authoritative interpretative community. It is, moreover, evident that a critic may be a member of a number of interpretative communities in the more or less "open" society of criticism, and at the very least he or she will be inwardly tempted or threatened by the discourses of certain significant others. The temptation and the threat posed by other discourses are both intellectual and institutional: they affect what Sartre would have called deep-seated ideological investments. These investments are at play in the dialectic of recognition among critics, and they bear upon ideal and material interests: books one has written, positions one has taken, one's appeal to graduate students, one's status in the profession, and so forth. Indeed, if the novel of contemporary criticism were to be written, it would look like a more or less bowdlerized version of *The Brothers Karamazov* with Wayne

Booth as Alyosha and Jacques Derrida as Ivan. I leave the casting of the other roles to the reader's imagination.

The problem for the historian of criticism would seem obvious: how does one write a history of a radically heterogeneous and internally dialogized "object"? One way to simplify one's task is to simplify one's story. A traditional plot may serve here as it has served throughout Western history. The present "time of troubles" may be perceived as an aberrant, babble-like era of confusion—a time of transition from a purer past to a repurified future. Different critical perspectives convert the plot into different stories. What they share is not only a convenient reduction of the complexities of the current critical scene, but an avoidance of inquiry into the sociocultural and political conditions that may actually be common to heterogeneous modes of criticism.

For some, perhaps for many critics, New Criticism existed in the purer past, dedicating itself steadfastly to the very ideal of purity— the purity of its literary object and of its own critical discourse about it. Of course, that object was internally complex, even ironic or paradoxical in structure, and it had to be wrested time and again from the crudely reductive incursions of "external" explanations. But it had its own "internal" autonomy and integrity that made the writing of the history of criticism that corresponded to it relatively unproblematic. As Wimsatt and Brooks put the point in the introduction to their *Literary Criticism: A Short History:*

> The first principle on which we would insist is that of con-
> tinuity and intelligibility in the history of literary argument.
> Plato has a bearing on Croce and Freud, and vice versa. Or, all
> three of these theorists are engaged with a common reality and
> hence engage one another through the medium of that reality
> and either come to terms or disagree. Literary problems occur
> not just because history produces them, but because literature
> is a thing of such and such a sort, showing such and such a re-
> lation to the rest of human experience. True, languages and
> cultures, times and places, differ widely. The literary historian

will always do well to nurse a certain skepticism about the thoroughness with which he may be penetrating the secret of his documents. But then he has to worry too about an opposite danger of being merely and overly skeptical.[3]

Today one might have second thoughts about metaphors of penetration. And it would be difficult to refer to "literature as a thing of such and such a sort, showing such and such a relation to the rest of human experience" and believe that such an indeterminate characterization could identify both a determinate literary object and a realm of literary criticism adequately corresponding to it. It might be crossing over into the hyperskeptical to observe that Wimsatt and Brooks wrote their history when the position of New Criticism seemed relatively firm but was in fact on the verge of multiple challenges. Their approach would seem to be that of proponents of a theoretical perspective that has already won its way and that has become "normalized" as a prevalent, perhaps a dominant, discourse. But, in retrospect, their words sound like the notes of Nero fiddling while you-know-what.

The specification of literary criticism as a field of discourse was to some significant extent related to its academic institutionalization in departments of literature, and New Criticism was one of the most forceful spokesmen for a discrete literary criticism with a solid institutional base. That base was primarily the Department of English and its attendant structures (periodicals, professional organizations, conferences). It is significant that a number of critical tendencies challenging New Criticism arose in other departments—departments such as French Literature and Comparative Literature, which were, for obvious reasons, more open to Continental influences and, for less obvious reasons, more marginalized in the university. Now, however, these tendencies have made waves in "mainstream" English departments in ways that both cause greater concern (insofar as the alien is within) and allow for

3. William K. Wimsatt, Jr., and Cleanth Brooks, *Literary Criticism: A Short History* (New York, 1957), p. vii.

processes of accommodation and naturalization. The discursive distance traveled from the early issues of *Diacritics* to *Critical Inquiry* may be taken as emblematic of this course of events.

The old New Criticism is still alive and well, but recent developments have not left its "discourse" unaffected. It is no longer a question of taking a territory from its former philological and positivistic inhabitants or of speaking from a seemingly secure sanctuary on occupied ground; it is rather a question of reasserting a tradition that is besieged and of shoring up a beleaguered fortress. The result may be vacillation, stridency, or a trenchant assertion of what Heidegger would see as the extreme form of modern metaphysics—the grounding of thought in subjective will. René Wellek is the only one in the recent past to have undertaken a panoramic survey of literary criticism over a number of centuries, and his explicit intention is to rehabilitate New Criticism.[4] But the defense he makes of his procedure is clearly more "willful" in tone than the self-assured and gentle suasiveness of Wimsatt and Brooks. In his "Reflections on My *History*" included in a book with the tell-tale title, *The Attack on Literature and Other Essays* (essays such as "The Fall of Literary History" and "Science, Pseudoscience, and Intuition in Recent Criticism"), Wellek asserts:

> Is there such a subject as "criticism," which can be isolated from other activities of man, and does it show some kind of unity, focus, and continuity? I have answered "yes" to both of those questions. . . . I am content to answer that criticism is any discourse on literature. It is thus clearly circumscribed by its theme, as many other sciences are, and the multitude of problems and approaches is precisely the topic of my book. One of its tasks is the sorting out of the different ways of defining and regarding the subject. A history of the concept of criticism, literature, and poetry is at the very center of the book. . . .
>
> We must think of criticism as a relatively independent ac-

4. René Wellek, *A History of Modern Criticism*, 4 vols. (New Haven, 1955–1965). A fifth volume is forthcoming.

tivity. No progress in any branch of learning has ever been made unless it was seen in comparative isolation, unless everything else was, to use the phenomenological terminology, "put into brackets." This isolation, which does not of course mean criticism for criticism's sake, is also a pragmatic imperative. If I had to discuss the relation of criticism to the practice of literature, I would have to examine, for instance, all the tragedies of Schiller or inquire whether Wordsworth actually wrote poetry in the common language of men. I would quickly abolish the unity of my subject matter, its continuity and development, and would make the history of criticism dissolve into the history of literature itself. Only by limiting the subject can we hope to master it.[5]

Dreams of mastery and apostrophes to progress aside, I would not object to the idea that research must be guided by a working definition of the relative specificity of literary criticism, however problematic and open to revision that definition may be. Nor would I object to the invocation of a variety of theoretical and practical considerations to defend that idea. It is, however, somewhat disconcerting to note that Wellek's history employs an approach that threatens to deprive it of any challenging problematic. Wellek provides an immensely erudite and readable dictionary of ideas about criticism in which he loosely combines New Critical presuppositions with a pastiche of other methods. In his *Attack on Literature and Other Essays,* Wellek vacillates somewhat in his defense of New Criticism, at one moment seeing its "presentism" as part of the "fall of literary history" while at another moment attempting to exonerate it from the charge that it was ahistorical.[6] His somewhat curious exoneration comprises three points. (1) New Criticism accepted "history" in the sense of providing necessary background information, for example, in the philological attempt to establish the meaning of words over time. (2) It saw the

5. René Wellek, *The Attack on Literature and Other Essays* (Chapel Hill, 1982), pp. 137–40.
6. Ibid., compare p. 67 and p. 87.

need for an internal history of poetry and literature that critically readjusted the hierarchy of works in the canon. (3) It confided in T. S. Eliot's revision of the traditional apocalyptic paradigm, a revision providing the following philosophy of history: a "dissociation of sensibility" in the modern period upset a once orderly and unified world that is to be rewon at least vicariously as the object of the poetic quest.[7] Wellek himself would probably not accept the first and third points as furnishing a notion of history in the relevant critical sense, but his own program is a displacement of the New Critical ideal of an internal history of literature. He calls for an internal history of literary criticism.

By confiding in the extrinsic/intrinsic dichotomy that played so vital a role in *The Theory of Literature*,[8] Wellek is able to avoid the more problematic issues in contemporary criticism or to resolve them through methodological fiat. He offers little indication of how the relation among texts, discourses, and contexts might be reformulated in a more cogent and self-critical fashion. Yet he does concede the following point: "The attempts at evolutionary history have failed. I myself have failed in *The History of Modern Criticism* to construe a convincing scheme of development. I discovered by experience that there is no evolution in the history of critical argument, that the history of criticism is rather a series of debates on recurrent concepts, on 'essentially contested concepts.'"[9]

Where then does one go if one abandons the hope for an evolutionary or developmental history of literary criticism along with the concept of a discrete object of study on which it relies? This question is exacerbated by the realization that the seeming alternative to unbroken continuity—continual breakage, either over time or space (dissociated periods or interpretative communities)—constitutes a simple reversal of perspectives that retains

7. Ibid., pp. 92–93.
8. René Wellek and Austin Warren, *The Theory of Literature* (New York, 1956).
9. *The Attack on Literature and Other Essays*, p. 77.

the basic assumption of unmarked purity or internal homogeneity within a discrete entity, class, or community of discourse. The latter view, theoretically affirmed in varying ways by certain historicists, Marxists, reader-response critics, and followers of Foucault (but often belied by their practice in interpretation), is itself well adjusted to a new rendition of the traditional apocalyptic paradigm: an all but inscrutable (magical, hermetic, religious, archaic, pre-Socratic, savage, medieval, pre-Renaissance—in any event, totally "other") discourse of the past was disrupted at some time by the rise of a scientific, secular, analytic, reductive, referential, logicist . . . discourse that dominates modernity; all we have at present are faint glimmerings of another global turning point in the history of discourse that will give content and meaning to what must be for us a blankly utopian future.[10] This scenario cannot be easily disparaged or dispelled, for it shapes the discourse of modernism which we still find compelling or even alluring. It implicitly underwrites the belief that the perhaps necessary passage through epistemological nihilism (often involving a lemming-like fascination for the aporetic "black holes" in discourse) may yet have a happy ending. But it can and, I think, should be contested by a different understanding of history that may even situate utopian desire in a somewhat different way.

One reason for an interest in history is that recent critical tendencies often seem as manifestly ahistorical as New Criticism, whether or not they may be interpreted, as Frank Lentricchia would have it, as occulted displacements of New Criticism itself.[11] What has sometimes characterized deconstructive criticism, including its important feminist variant, is an unmediated combination of micrological readings of texts or textual fragments and grander implications of an extremely allusive sort. The result is suggestive of a gallery of delicate miniatures whose focus is offset by allegorical atmospheric effects. Paul de Man has insisted that

10. For a recent and extremely learned rendition of this view, see Timothy J. Reiss, *The Discourse of Modernism* (Ithaca, 1982).
11. Frank Lentricchia, *After the New Criticism* (Chicago, 1980).

"one has to pretend to read . . . ahistorically, the first and necessary condition if there is to be any expectation of ever arriving at a somewhat reliable history."[12]

The obvious difficulty is that the "expectation of ever arriving at a somewhat reliable history" may be deferred indefinitely. I do not read de Man as advocating an intransigently unworldly theory devoid of interest in history, but rather as contending that certain approaches to reading enable one to pose the problem of history in a manner that places in question interpretative maneuvers prevalent among historians and, at times, even among literary critics. Among these maneuvers, I would mention the one whereby an ill-defined notion of "the historical context" is constituted as an external, extra-discursive ground and assumed to solve all basic problems in interpretation, including those that may have been disclosed by one's own reading of a text. (Unexamined contextualism is so ingrained as an explanatory gesture in historiography that it might almost be termed "cracker-barrel logocentrism.") I would take de Man's remark to imply that critical reading, on the contrary, requires an inquiry into both the conditions of possibility of history and the way those conditions are enacted or contorted in actual historical processes. With reference to the work of Derrida, the principal condition of history would be the movement of repetition with difference. In the somewhat analogous dimension of de Man's work, it would be the unsettling movement through which an insight or, indeed, a blank apprehension of "unreadability," even of sheer materiality, is necessarily accommodated as it relapses into a kind of compromise formation that may be required for ordinary life and thought. This view itself opens the possibility of rethinking the relation between texts and contexts in a manner that addresses the issue of writing the history of radically heterogeneous objects.

Derrida has offered an "example" of such a history in his

12. Paul de Man, "The Epistemology of Metaphor," in Sheldon Sacks, ed., *On Metaphor* (Chicago, 1979), p. 14.

treatment of the texts that both constitute and subvert the larger
context that we somewhat deceptively call "the metaphysical tradition." His history of this tangled tradition is, moreover, not
simply regional, insofar as metaphysical concepts and oppositions
affect conceptualization elsewhere. Even more generally, Derrida's
approach may be taken to indicate that there are good reasons for
reading Eliot or Frye along with Nietzsche, Freud, Durkheim, or
Marx because literary criticism must be related to other modes of
criticism—social, cultural, and political—on both intellectual and
institutional levels. Indeed, as I have already intimated, Derrida
shakes or "solicits" the metaphysical foundations of historiography itself by elaborating a notion of temporality that is the story of
neither continuity nor discontinuity and that disrupts the classical
opposition between the particular or unique and the universal or
intemporal. His account is one wherein repetition and change,
iteration and alteration, occur together over (or as) time. Temporality as repetition with change also situates the critic in a
transferential relation to the "object" of study; it denies the possibility of total mastery but it also opens that of a more informed
and self-critical "dialogue" or interchange with the past. (One
might also observe that a notion of periodicity tends to displace
that of periodization.) In this respect, one might argue that micrological readings are in and of themselves historical readings if they
are undertaken in a certain way, and they counteract the deceptively vatic pretensions of macrological histories. This argument is
convincing within limits. But it does not negate the interest or the
desirability of a more sustained effort to relate certain readings to a
reconceptualization of historical processes, including the very relation between texts and their contexts of writing and reception. The
result of this effort might be a transformed notion of "intertex-
tuality" that would both test the limits of the textual metaphor and
have more evident political effects. One such effect would be an
attempt to relate the problems of undecidability and aporia to the
issue of discursive carnivalization as a mode in which irreconcila-
ble but impure differences are played out and discursive "black

holes" are somehow negotiated. Carnivalization in this sense might emerge as a process that is itself both "contestatory" and "recuperative" or accommodating in ways that would necessarily vary with specific historical and social conditions. The broader issue would be how to articulate the reading of texts and contexts, where Derrida has made some of the most significant overtures, with the critique of society and culture, where Marx's own highly carnivalized texts provide models still worthy of emulation. In this respect, it is noteworthy that the dimension of the texts of both Derrida and Marx that have perhaps had the least "influence" upon those working with reference to them is their admittedly different inflections of the carnivalesque. Indeed the ironic story of Derrida's "impact" or "reception" involves a joke of sorts. Derrida has not only rehabilitated liminal or marginal phenomena in a forceful fashion that radically undermines the tendency to victimize or "scapegoat" them. (This is, I think, one of the most important institutional implications of deconstruction.) At least on an intellectual level, he has also managed to convert numerous upright, respectable scholars into dispossessed, wandering Jews or itinerant Franciscans ("God's jugglers," as Saint Francis himself called them). Yet there has been relatively little exploration of the way Derrida has fulfilled Nietzsche's prophecy that the originality of the future might lie in laughter, in the inventions of "parodists of world history and God's buffoons."[13]

I am not urging the simple (and quite "unDerridean") substitution of a comic or a farcical for a tragic "vision" of history. Nor am I underemphasizing the difficulty of relating a "critique" of critical decisions on a foundational level (Derrida's project) to an informed and decisive critique of political, social, and economic institutions (Marx's project). But I am signaling the importance of

13. Friedrich Nietzsche, *Beyond Good and Evil*, trans. Walter Kaufmann (New York, 1966), p. 150. For a discussion of the carnivalesque in Marx, see Dominick LaCapra, "Reading Marx: The Case of *The Eighteenth Brumaire*" and "Bakhtin, Marxism, and the Carnivalesque," in *Rethinking Intellectual History: Texts, Contexts, Language* (Ithaca, 1983).

this endeavor—an endeavor that would involve both a transformation of the way we relate to the marginal and an attempt to undo the "scapegoat mechanism" which relies on a logic of pure binary oppositions. And I am suggesting that it could lead to a different apprehension of what are often formulated in extremely restricted terms as formal contradictions between absolutely incompatible propositions, postulates, and positions. The aporia (or the *mise en abyme*) brings one face-to-face with faceless anxiety, but it may also trace the thin line that scarcely separates anxiety from laughter. In the latter respect, the aporia is a mode of carnivalesque uncrowning. Indeed, as Bakhtin indicates, the carnivalesque may itself assume the role of a "realistic" utopia that characterizes not society as a whole, immobilized in a perfect moment, but rather a way of life and thought that alternates, more or less rhythmically and controversially, with workaday practices and procedures. It may also be the wake-like counterpart of the irreducibly tragic aspects of existence that overly reductive, logic-chopping analyses tend to obliterate. One obvious problem, however, is how carnivalesque forms, which are weak or questionable in modern society, may be developed and related to problematic distinctions instead of rigidly authoritarian hierarchies.

In more specific and pragmatic terms, my comments would imply the importance, in writing the history of criticism, of attempting to trace in precise terms the configurations of repetition and change over time—the variations in the way the "same" problems are debated as well as in the way institutional, ideological, and political issues are at stake in those debates.[14] The very manner in which one wrote this history would perforce reenact and to some extent transform the discursive configuration in

14. One noteworthy "example" of this type of history of criticism is *L'absolu littéraire: théorie de la littérature du romantisme allemand,* by Philippe Lacoue-Labarthe and Jean-Luc Nancy (Paris, 1978). Here the concerns of the Schlegel circle are seen as opening up a "romantic" problematic with which criticism is still trying to come to terms today. The interweaving of translations of texts and commentary on them is undertaken with an active awareness of the transferential problem in relating to a *passé* that is not *dépassé.*

which debates take place at present. It would also raise the possibility of "generalizing" within cases, that is, of writing about more or less delimited problems with a sensitivity to their broader resonance and their bearing upon contemporary controversies. The way this possibility is actualized may give seemingly circumscribed studies greater comparative significance than ostensibly comparative endeavors or panoramic surveys with a "big band" sound. In this sense, for example, there would be a point to taking up again Lentricchia's project of relating Derrida to Continental figures he "rewrites," such as Heidegger and Freud, and then attempting to plot variations in the "Americanization" of deconstruction. The "theme" guiding this regional history of criticism would be that of "iteration-alteration," and the pertinent discursive and institutional contexts of writing and reception would have to be specified. Here it would be astounding if New Criticism were not a pertinent reference point in the American reception of Derrida, although the nature of its displacement would entail a more complex and divided story than Lentricchia's, one including an account of what resists ready-made caricature in the critical practice of the New Critics themselves.

I would like to end on an institutional note, a somewhat dissonant note insofar as there is no simple coincidence between the intellectual and institutional aspects of discursive commitments. Here as elsewhere the critic may speak with a forked tongue. In empirical fact, the institutional impact of contemporary critical controversy may be less pronounced than one might expect, and its theoretical implications for the restructuring of institutions are moot.

Especially when viewed with a sense of anthropological distance, the society of critics may often resemble a preview for a Heideggerian soap opera entitled "As the World Worlds." A deconstructive or a reader-response critic may well behave institutionally in the same way as his old New Critical or neo-Aristotelian neighbor—iterations outweighing alterations and internal dialogization tending toward a common denominator. The category of literary criticism may be questioned, but literary critics may continue to band together in subgroups and networks, cultivate an *esprit de cénacle,* cite primarily the work of others in their circle, disseminate daisy-chains of articles on "in" topics, and refer clannishly to the same small set of totemic "superstars." Conferences may continue to remind one of the last scene in "Casablanca," where Louis tells his associates to "round up the usual suspects." And an occasional outsider may be invited as a friendly "other" or a convenient scapegoat. The thoroughgoing subversion of all existing categories and the apprehensive intimation of an unknowable utopian future both agitate discourse and facilitate a return to institutional practice as usual.

There is an important sense in which thought requires utopian agitation, even when that agitation threatens to be sterile, and a negative absolute may be better than a blandly positivistic dismissal of all metaphysical pathos. In their bearing upon practice, however, absolutes are postulated not to be fully realized but to be countered, and the way they are countered does affect both discourse and institutions. I have indicated that the most immediate problem raised for academics by "criticism" today may be the bearing of recent developments on established disciplines and newer institutional possibilities. Here the point may not be to try to eliminate the anxiety caused by the elusiveness of a clear and distinct object of inquiry that lends an identity to one's field or discipline; it may be to allow that anxiety to affect institutional practice and discourse in ways that enable people to pursue issues into eccentric spaces or disconcerting "temporalities." Institutions at present react rather differently to this anxiety which is, I think, a necessary component of contemporary research in the humanities and social sciences. The formula at my own university is relatively simple. One person, whatever his or her departmental affiliation, may teach just about anything (subject, of course, to the sanction of tenure). Two people team-teaching a course enjoy a similar latitude. Three people or more and you have a conspiracy. Hence the absence of institutionalized interdisciplinary programs in the humanities. But the problematization of the category of literary criticism is after all not new; its constitution as a seemingly discrete entity was. The past offers its own modes of discursive interaction that in good measure still have to be charted.

I have intimated only in a general way how the charting of these variations in terms of a critical dialogue between past and present would require the attempt to relate literary criticism as an institution and a discursive practice to other institutions and discursive practices while remaining open to the possibility that one's findings might require the reconceptualization of the very terms and articulations with which one began. Recent doubts about what counts as "literary" or as relevant to literary criticism may be an indication that more critical concepts are needed to understand the present condition of the discipline and its course in recent history alone. The very constitution of literary criticism as a discipline depended upon a network of inclusions and exclusions (generally conceived in terms of the establishment of a "canon") and the insertion of the discipline into an institutional matrix. This development took place within a larger process of differentiation— indeed in certain respects a splitting—of culture into elite, popular, official, and "mass" sectors or areas, which were themselves subject to further internal differentiation and division. At this point, I would simply note the invasive importance of mass culture in the modern period. "Mass" culture may be defined as the process not only whereby culture is constituted as a commodity but wherein the commodity-status of the artifact threatens to assume hegemony over it. With reference to best-sellers, film, and television, the degree of capital investment in the artifact virtually assures the priority of its status as a commodity. But even pockets of popular culture (workers, peasants, subcultures) have been threatened by disintegration or decisive modification under the impact of commodification and related processes. And elite culture itself is not immune to commodifying processes. One naturally thinks of the highly inaccessible text that may become a best-seller in part through its conversion into "symbolic capital" that reinforces social prestige and power. But one might also think of the manner in which the transmission of elite culture in the university is subject to the pressure of both official culture (government funding and the often related policies of private funding agencies) and the need to package things in a way that will "appeal to the kids."

The heterogeneous approaches to literary criticism I have mentioned thus far are by and large components of one segment of elite culture affiliated with the university and related institutions—an elite culture often oblivious to its implication in a larger sociocultural and political matrix. From a larger perspective, the very heterogeneity of this segment of elite culture may appear to be a relatively superficial phenomenon, for even critics who contest this elite status typically do so in terms inaccessible—or of little interest—to groups outside the elite. Even when their arguments legitimate the study of popular and "mass" culture within a university setting, reject qualitative distinctions among—or even within—levels of culture as rank elitist prejudice, and denigrate the importance of elite culture and its bearers in terms that often amount, at the very least, to methodological scapegoating, they nonetheless continue to address themselves primarily if not exclusively to other members of an elite.

To say this is not to pander to a morbid delight in the aporias of current institutional life. It is to stress the problem of sociocultural differentiation and the difficulty of addressing it in historical and critical terms. Here I would mention two complementary temptations. The first is the reinforcement of a snobbish, suspect elitism, e.g., by simply writing off popular and "mass" culture and defending the inviolate purity of a "canon"—or, for that matter, by indulging a facile equation of political radicalism and formal innovation in all its guises and under all conditions.[15] The second is the turn to uncritical populism that vociferously promotes the study of

15. The *carte blanche* endorsement of formal experimentation, often seen as necessarily allied with political radicalism, has been characteristic of recent French critics such as Roland Barthes, Julia Kristeva, and Jean-François Lyotard.

"noncanonical" artifacts—best-sellers, Grub Street literature, film, television—whose assimilation into a manipulative "mass" culture is either positivistically chronicled or caustically condemned.[16] Uncritical populists may even ignore the fact that the greatest critics of a "canon," such as Walter Benjamin, developed their critical abilities in large part through a careful reading of canonical texts—a fact that ought to be taken to indicate that the point is not to destroy the canon but to read it in noncanonical ways, both by bringing out how its texts resist, contest, and even subvert hegemonic forces they may also affirm and by relating it critically to artifacts and contexts often deemed irrelevant to it. This reading may play at least a small part in the formation of habits of thought necessary for any desirable reconstruction of culture and the institution of criticism itself. It may thus provide

16. The attempt to privilege more "representative" literature has become widespread in both literary criticism and historiography, and it is often based on uncritical populism that involves methodological scapegoating of intellectuals and their artifacts. Leslie Fiedler is perhaps the best-known defender of a reliance on sure-fire techniques in mass-market literature, and his free-wheeling, mock-ironic style pokes fun at the commodity system while refraining from a critique of its effects. But even more militantly political critics can give dubious reasons in defending the need for inquiry into best-selling or widely read literature. In trying to bolster his case for worldly criticism, Edward Said quotes this passage by Robert Darnton: "Much of what passes today as 18th century French literature wasn't much read by Frenchmen in the 18th century. . . . We suffer from an arbitrary notion of literary history as a canon of classics, one which was developed by professors of literature in the 19th and 20th centuries—while in fact what people of the 18th century were reading was very different. By studying the publisher's accounts and papers at [the Société Typographique de Neuchâtel] I've been able to construct a kind of bestseller list of pre-revolutionary France, and it doesn't look anything like the reading lists passed out in classrooms today." (Quoted by Edward Said, "Opponents, Audiences, Constituencies, and Community," *Critical Inquiry* 9 [September 1982]: 17.) Darnton's statement that a reconstructed bestseller list of eighteenth-century France does not coincide with a canon of classics should occasion as little surprise as the observation that today Louis L'Amour has more readers than James Joyce. There is clearly an important place for the social history of ideas, but it need not imply a tendentious identification of the historically significant with the collectively representative or the empirically effective. The problem for research is how to work out relations among perspectives on the past that do not blindly replicate the splits and animosities prevailing in the object of study.

some insight into alternative possibilities that are generally left a total blank by those who confine themselves to a sociological critique of existing structures or a blind faith in some collective cultural "production" of the future.[17]

I have no synoptic formula for resolving the various problems I have tried to raise. I would simply end by saying that what emerges from my discussion is the necessity and the difficulty of linking the history of criticism to criticism itself—criticism that is not only literary but sociocultural and political as well. Another way to state this point is to reiterate the need to come to terms with the problem of transference in the relation between past and present. In this respect, the practice of the critic would have to engage the issue of its own situation in the complex intellectual and institutional network formed by elite, official, popular, and "mass" (or commodified) culture. Countering the temptation to replicate in one's own protocols of interpretation some of the most questionable features of cultural history is for the critic writing the history of criticism—or indeed any form of history—an endeavor that is substantive and self-reflexive at the same time.

17. See the extremely useful analysis in Peter Uwe Hohendahl, *The Institution of Criticism* (Ithaca, 1982). Hohendahl, however, at times seems to relegate textual literary criticism to an anachronistic "liberal" ideology and to advocate a wholesale conversion of the discipline into a critical sociology of the institution of literature in capitalistic society. Fredric Jameson in *The Political Unconscious* (Ithaca, 1981) combines a wide-ranging historical and cultural critique of literature with utopian faith that the "empty chair" he leaves for a substantive political culture will be filled by "some as yet unrealized, collective, and decentered cultural production of the future, beyond realism and modernism alike" (p. 11).

5

History and the Novel

It is not exactly a matter of free choice whether or not a cultural historian shall be a literary critic, nor is it open to him to let his virtuous political and social opinions do duty for percipience.

LIONEL TRILLING, *The Liberal Imagination*

ONE might begin with the question: why should a professional historian bother to read novels? The sad fact is that a number of historians at present would actually take this as a real question. They might well enjoy reading novels in their "free" or "leisure" time, but they would be hard pressed to see the novel as playing a part in their professional life. Even intellectual historians who have not totally redefined their activity as a function of social history might nonetheless exclude or downplay the significance of the novel in their research and teaching. This being the case, it may be necessary to belabor what should be obvious before broaching the more significant question: how should one read novels in history?

Georg Lukács argued that the novel was *the* genre of the bourgeois epoch. It presented one with a problematic hero whose ideals were more or less systematically contradicted by social reality, and the great critical realists such as Balzac or Tolstoy might in their novels disclose dimensions of contemporary history that challenged their own explicit ideologies. From a rather different perspective, Mikhail Bakhtin saw the novel as the epitome of modern culture and the most pronounced form of "dialogized" language use in general. In the case of Dostoevsky, he referred to the polyphonic novel wherein the author's voice is one contestant in a larger field of forces, and in discussing Rabelais he developed further his idea of grotesque realism in the novel as the medium for carnivalized uses of language. More generally, for Bakhtin the novel was a genre that tested the limits of generic classification and continually renewed itself by incorporating other genres and social usages in an active interchange of perspectives and voices. In a somewhat similar vein, Lionel Trilling has remarked:

> For our time the most effective agent of the moral imagination has been the novel of the last two hundred years. It was never, either aesthetically or morally, a perfect form and its faults and failures can be quickly enumerated. But its greatness and its practical usefulness lay in its unremitting work of involving the reader himself in the moral life, inviting him to put his own motives under examination, suggesting that reality is not as his conventional education has led him to see it. It taught us, as no other genre ever did, the extent of human variety and the value of this variety. It was the literary form to which the emotions of understanding and forgiveness were indigenous, as if by the definition of the form itself.[1]

Even if one were to characterize the appraisals of these theorists as effective rhetorical motivations for their own work, it is far from hyperbolic to observe that the novel is one very important mode of writing in the modern period. In this sense, there is something suspect about an approach to history—and particularly to intellectual history—that does not address the novel both as an object of study and self-reflexively as a way of coming to terms with problems in modern history itself. These considerations of course raise the question of narrative in the novel and in historiography as well.

1. *The Liberal Imagination* (1940; New York, 1950), p. 222.

Since the end of the nineteenth century, historians have been attracted by a scientific, at times even a positivistic, model of research. This model often involves borrowings from the social sciences. Historians stressing the importance of close working relations with the social sciences may see fields such as literary criticism and philosophy as quite alien. The novel itself becomes little more than questionable "literary" evidence, and an interest in literature (or philosophy) that goes beyond narrowly documentary limits is a tell-tale sign that one is not really doing history. (The assertion that something is not history usually conceals a major premise and a conclusion: I am a historian. Therefore, I do not have to be concerned with it.)

Until recently, historians looking to the social sciences for guidance might denigrate the role of narrative in history and emphasize the need to subject "data" to analysis, hypothesis-formation, and model-building in the interest of elaborating valid explanations of historical phenomena. If the "artistic" side of history entered the picture at all, it would be through the narrow gate of a rather perfunctory idea of "good style" in writing that was accessible to the proverbial "generally educated person." "Good style," when it did not simply occult the problem of "voice," restricted the historian to an "objective" description and analysis of facts. "Objectivity" implied the dominance of an impersonal or "voiceless" voice, and "subjective" interventions (marked by the use of the first-person pronoun) had to be largely confined to a preface or conclusion. More occasional interventions of "non-objective" tendencies in the body of the historical text threatened to disrupt established rules of decorum, and anything approximating a more complex "dialogue" between past and present (or historian and "documentary" evidence) seemed to be ruled out *ab initio*.

Social historians have of course been particularly notable exponents of a scientific and at times a positivistic idea of history. Until a short time ago, the influential *Annales* school tended to view narrative as superficial, to stress a social-scientific conception of "serious" history with an emphasis upon statistical series and exhaustive archival research, and to hold forth the ideal of a "total history" in which social history had the privileged position of basic ground or essential indicator of fundamental reality. One often heard—and still occasionally hears—phrases such as "the need to root problems in social reality." Total history itself might serve as a Trojan horse for a social metaphysic in the understanding of the past and a pretension to preeminence in the present organization of the historical profession.

In the more immediate past, the *Annales* school has become somewhat less dogmatic and evangelical in its assumptions, at least among its more self-conscious and self-critical affiliates.[2] The idea of a total history has been either shifted in the direction of a more problematic general history or radically contested in the name of a "splintered" or decentered history. Here one perhaps has not alternatives but indications of the need for historians to attend to the interaction between order and challenges to it both in the past and in one's own discourse in addressing the past. In any case, the often concealed metaphysical belief that society is the ultimate ground of all historical research has at least been rendered more flexible by an awareness of the role of symbolic systems and signifying practices in the formation of society itself. And narrative has been rehabilitated as a way of representing the past.

The partial return to narrative and the insistence on the problem of "symbolic meaning" may, however, indicate certain respects in which older conceptions of history as (empirical-analytic) science and as (narrative) art were not so far apart in basic assumptions, and they may simultaneously disclose the limitations of newer developments in social history in general. Older scientific and narrative approaches were coordinate ways of coding or organiz-

2. See, for example, the appraisal in Roger Chartier, "Intellectual History or Sociocultural History? The French Trajectories," in Dominick LaCapra and Steven L. Kaplan, eds., *Modern European Intellectual History: Reappraisals and New Perspectives* (Ithaca, 1982), pp. 13–46. See also the works of Michel de Certeau, which are especially significant for historians when they are read as revisions of prominent tendencies of the *Annales* school. (It would of course take a separate study to treat the billowing generosity of Fernand Braudel's thought.)

ing the same facts, and they might share a number of significant features: a basically documentary conception of literature as part of the historical record; a suspicion of critical self-reflection as injurious to the historian's craft; and an unproblematic idea of the historian's use of language that avoids or represses significant aspects of an exchange with the past, including the role of "internally dialogized" styles in history that involve self-questioning, humor, stylization, irony, parody, and self-parody. The recent turn to the problem of "symbolic meaning" itself often rests on an oversimplified idea of language use—one in which the term "social," for example, is understood not as a problematic qualifier but as an essential or constitutive definer of "meaning." One practical result is the elimination or the homogenization of exceptional, contestatory, or even uncanny uses of language in history as well as the attendant marginalization of an approach to intellectual history that is sensitive to these uses. And the "narrative" to which a partial return has been made is itself rather traditional in nature.

Take, for example, a study such as Emmanuel Le Roy Ladurie's *Montaillou* (1975)—a study hailed both by professional historians and by the general public. It is a beautifully composed but highly conventional narrative. It is effective because it combines ostensibly well-documented research and a traditional story (at times a romance) form in ways that appear to be highly plausible and lifelike. In the manner in which it uses an inquisition register as a simple source for facts rather than a complex text having problematic relations to other sociocultural processes, it might, however, almost be termed precritical.

Outside the orbit of the *Annales* school, Garrett Mattingly's *The Armada* (1959) is often taken as a paradigm of modern narrative history. In its basic approach to story-telling, it belongs to the unproblematic world shared by *Montaillou*, for it is a lovely old-style tale. It almost makes you believe that England still rules the seas of traditional narrative and daily defeats the invading armadas that besiege traditional story-telling in other waters, such as those navigated by the modern novel.

Certain professional historians and social scientists, trying to check the tendency of traditional narrative to romanticize events (a tendency that may be an inevitable consequence of the imaginative reconstruction of "lived experience" on the basis of limited documentation), make narrative as objective and documentary-like as possible. In its more extreme form, this kind of history provides the familiar, dull series of dry and noncommittal declarative sentences in the third person and the past tense. But it may reach disconcerting extremes of impersonal reportage that convert it into an unselfconscious imitation of techniques used parodically by novelists such as Flaubert. I offer for its stylistic interest a paragraph from the first chapter of a work on Durkheim, a chapter entitled, appropriately enough, "Childhood." (In brackets I include the author's footnotes.)

> David Émile Durkheim was born on 15 April 1858 at Épinal, capital town of the department of Vosges, in Lorraine. His father, Moïse Durkheim, had been the rabbi of Épinal since the 1830s and was Chief Rabbi of the Vosges and Haute-Marne; his grandfather, Israël David Durkheim, had been a rabbi in Mutzig (Alsace), as also had his great-grandfather Simon Simon, appointed in 1784. His mother, Mélanie *née* Isidor, was the daughter of a trader in beer (or horses). He grew up within the confines of a close-knit, orthodox and traditional Jewish family, part of the long-established Jewish community of Alsace-Lorraine that was notable for providing France with many army officers and civil servants at the end of the nineteenth century. [1. See Aubéry, P., *Milieux juifs de la France contemporaine* (2nd edn, Paris, 1962), p. 61, and Anchel, R., *Les juifs en France* (Paris, 1946), p. 18. See Appendix G in Lukes, 1968b, for a reproduction of Durkheim's family tree, which gives a striking picture of a sample of this community's upward social mobility over six generations.] Durkheim, however, was destined for the rabbinate and his early education was directed to that end: he studied for a time at a rabbinical school. [2. M. Étienne Halphen, personal communication.] Yet he soon decided, while still a schoolboy, not to follow the

family   tradition.   [3.   M.   Georges   Davy,   personal
communication.]3

Everyone has at some time written a similar passage, but this one
seems to be a curiously displaced visitor from the pages of *Bouvard
et Pécuchet*. It includes many precious moments: the disorienting
series of "begats" forming a *cortège* after Durkheim's name; the
digressive reference to army officers and civil servants followed by
doubly digressive, erudite references; the use of the colon to introduce an anticlimactic tautology; the invocation of "personal com-
munications" to authenticate facts that are fairly well known and
available in published sources. (The intriguing equivalence between beer and horses is, by the way, never explained, and it
creates a fantastic afterglow of indeterminacy in the text.)

At least for shock effect, one might juxtapose the above-quoted
passage with a remarkably different account. Here is the last entry
in Virginia Woolf's diary:

> Just back from L's speech at Brighton. Like a foreign town: the
> first spring day. Women sitting on seats. A pretty hat in a tea
> shop—how fashion revives the eye! And the shell-encrusted
> old women, rouged, decked, cadaverous at the tea shop. No: I
> intend no introspection. I mark Henry James' sentence: ob-
> serve perpetually. Observe the oncome of age. Observe greed.
> Observe my own despondency. By that means it becomes
> serviceable. Or so I hope. I insist upon spending this time to the
> best advantage. I will go down with my colours flying. This, I
> see, verges on introspection; but doesn't quite fall in. Suppose I
> bought a ticket at the Museum; biked in daily and read history.
> Suppose I selected one dominant figure in every age and wrote
> round and about. Occupation is essential. And now with some
> pleasure I find that it's seven; and must cook dinner. Haddock
> and sausage meat. I think it is true that one gains a certain hold
> on sausage and haddock by writing them down.4

3. Steven Lukes, *Emile Durkheim: His Life and Work* (London, 1973), p. 1.
4. Virginia Woolf, *A Writer's Diary*, ed. with an intro. by Leonard Woolf (New
York and London, 1953), p. 351.

This passage produces a very different sensation from the one I quoted earlier, especially if one knows its existential sequel. But among the shock effects created by Virginia Woolf's diary is the fact that it really does not seem to deliver the documentary perspective on the author's life that readers with conventional leanings might expect from it. It seems to depict a "lived reality" and a way of transcribing it that are uncomfortably close to what one finds in Woolf's novels. And language in those novels does things that often seem terribly unlike the doings of language in contemporaneous historiography.

Here one point is particularly significant. In the nineteenth century, the novel and narrative history often exhibited noteworthy parallels. Masters of narrative could be found in both areas of prose discourse. Historians such as Michelet, Carlyle, and Macaulay were great narrators and might even compete with novelists for audiences. At times, in the case of Carlyle for example, historians might even employ rather "experimental" forms. (I am thinking especially of the uproarious intellectual history *cum* spiritual autobiography one finds in *Sartor Resartus*.) Toward the end of the nineteenth century, there is by contrast a parting of the ways in historical and novelistic narrative. Narrative in history tends, with some exceptions, to remain set in its nineteenth-century ways. Developments in narrative history tend to be on the "scientific" level of better documentation and data collection, and in line with these developments Ranke is probably the most widely emulated narrative historian. There is relatively little self-consciousness about the problem of voice or point of view; the narrator tends to be omniscient and to rely on the convention of unity not only of narrative voice but between narrative and authorial voice; and the story is typically organized in accordance with a chronologically arranged, beginning-middle-end structure.

To illustrate the latter point, one might refer to H. Stuart Hughes's procedure in *Consciousness and Society* (1958). Hughes defines his period of study from 1890 to 1930 in terms of a generational cluster of genius—a group of intellectuals who shared

in a neo-idealist critique of positivism. It is quite true that the turn
of the century witnessed a critical response to the application of
narrowly scientific methods to the study of human beings, and a
number of figures stressed the importance of meaning, interpretation, and values in the human sciences. But a critique of positivism
in this sense had already been undertaken in powerful forms before
1890 by figures such as Nietzsche and Kierkegaard, for example,
and this critique remained a notable reference point after 1890. In
the period from 1890 to 1930, as Hughes himself acknowledges,
positivistic strains continued to be pronounced in the works of
figures such as Durkheim and Freud. And the problematic relations between positivism and idealism still concerned thinkers after
1930. More significant, perhaps, some of the most important
thinkers in the modern period questioned the theoretical cogency
of certain binary oppositions—oppositions such as that between
positivism and idealism upon which Hughes himself relies. Here
the name of Heidegger is of obvious relevance. The more general
point is that Hughes in addressing what he takes to be the most
critically self-reflective thought of the modern period relies rather
uncritically on standard concepts and assumptions, notably a
method of periodization that provides a chronological frame for a
conventional, untroubled narrative. And instead of justifying periodization on unobjectionable pragmatic grounds, he tries to invest
it with the kind of theoretical weight it cannot really bear. What
tends to be obscured in the process is the role of something Hughes
himself recognizes as crucial: the way in which objective knowledge of the past, furnished by procedures such as periodization, is
supplemented by what Freud would have called a transferential
relation to the object of study—one whereby the problems we
investigate find their displaced analogues in our account of them.

  In the novel since Flaubert, one has witnessed by contrast a
tremendous explosion of exploratory approaches to narrative. It
may not be possible or even desirable to have comparable stylistic
and formal mutations in historiography. (The work of Foucault,
notably his compelling attempt to render the pathos of a broken

dialogue between reason and unreason in *Folie et déraison: histoire de la folie à l'âge classique,* indicates some of the possibilities and dangers of very experimental historical narrative.) But certain modifications and initiatives may be more possible and desirable than one would infer from prevalent if not dominant tendencies in professional historiography and social science. Point of view or narrative perspective, for example, can become more of an issue when one attempts to come to terms with a transferential relation to the past. The obvious danger is that an experimental account, to the extent that it is inventive in its interpretations, may become "projective" (in the ordinary sense of the term). But transference is something more and, in crucial respects, something other than being too inventive or construing the object in terms of one's own concerns. Uncritical transference may indeed involve imputing to the "other" traits one refuses to recognize in oneself. But, in this more pointed sense, a conventional account may be quite "projective." And what is most projective is the avoidance of argument by directing the charge of projection against an interpretation or an entire interpretative orientation with which one disagrees for reasons that remain unstated and unexamined. The question is not whether transference takes place; it is how it takes place and what the nature of the ensuing interchange with the "object" is and should be. Purely objectivist or positivistic postures involve the denial or negation of transference, and they may function to conceal the mechanism at work when one makes a scapegoat of the other—a mechanism that may at least be counteracted through a more critical and self-critical exchange.

One aspect of a transferential and dialogical relation to the past returns us to the question of how one is to read novels in history. And it displaces our focus from analogies between the novel and history to the question of the relation between historiography and literary criticism. For a crucial issue at this juncture is that of alternatives to narrowly documentary or positivistic uses of literary texts. Indeed there may even be difficulties in the treatment of any document purely and simply as a source for facts about the past rather than as a text that also supplements or reworks what it "represents."

If the novel is read at all in history, it is typically because it may be employed as a source telling us something factual about the past. Its value is in its referential functions—the way it serves as a window on life or developments in the past. The historian's focus is, accordingly, on the content of the novel—its representation of social life, its characters, its themes, and so forth. In a word, the novel is pertinent to historical research to the extent that it may be converted into useful knowledge or information. For example, *The Red and the Black* informs us about social and political tensions in early nineteenth-century France as well as about the problems of an upwardly mobile young man from the provinces. *Madame Bovary* tells us about longer-term trends in provincial society and the frustrations of a woman who is not adapted to its demands. Balzac is of course a favorite novelist from a documentary perspective because he manifestly tried to provide a panoramic view of contemporary life and explicitly compared the novel to social science. (The question of course is the extent to which his novelistic practice, often involving a hyperbolic and contestatory inflation of social "realities," conformed to his self-interpretation—indeed whether his famous statement in the preface to *La comédie humaine* had a narrowly representational meaning. Balzac asserted that he wanted to compete with civil society—*faire concurrence à l'état civil*—not simply "represent" it.)

It has become increasingly evident that a restricted documentary use of novels, such as the one made by Louis Chevalier for example, encounters serious problems.[5] It typically engenders a histor-

---

5. See Chevalier's *Classes laborieuses et classes dangereuses* (Paris, 1958). What Chevalier writes of Eugène Sue's *Les mystères de Paris* is typical of his approach to reading novels in general: "The social importance of this novel, like that of other great novels of the time, comes from the fact that their authors describe a society and an epoch to which they belong. . . . The extraordinary authenticity of *Les mystères de Paris*, like that of *Les misérables*, comes from the fact that these works passively register the demographic and economic evolutions that we have evoked. They are of their time and can do nothing other than attribute to the society they

ical narrative that is less self-critical and probing than the literary narratives for which it tries to account. And it provides too simple an answer to the question of the relation between the use of language in literature and signifying practices in the rest of society and culture. In the process, it makes literature either redundant or purely suggestive (hence, not "serious").

Literature becomes redundant when it tells us what can be gleaned from other documentary sources. In this sense, literature is paradoxically most superfluous when it seems to provide us with the most "useful" and "reputable" information, for it must simply replicate or confirm what can be found in more literal documents such as police reports. (I bracket in passing the question of whether police reports require a "textual" reading, for example, in terms of fantasies about conspiracies against public order and desires for comprehensive administrative control of society.) Literature is merely suggestive, for example, in giving us a "feel" for life in the past, when its information cannot be checked against other sources. It must then be given second-class status in historical scholarship, although what cannot be checked may bear upon some of the most significant and subtle processes in life.

We seem to have arrived at an impasse that signals the need for an alternative approach to literature. Here it may be noted that the formalistic idea of a text as a self-enclosed cosmos making use of purely literary devices is not an alternative, nor is any simple combination of documentary and formalistic methods. In fact documentary and formalistic reductions of texts are complementary gestures resting on common assumptions. They rely on the binary opposition between the content and the form of a text, and

---

describe the characteristics that their authors know in the same manner in which they were known at the same moment by the most uncultivated [*incultes*] inhabitants of the city" (pp. 514–15; my translation). It is striking to note that the social historian's notion of "authenticity" is the exact opposite of that developed by Heidegger in *Being and Time*. Its unqualified application to untutored or popular classes is, moreover, open to question, for it seems to imply that critical readings of texts are impossible among the "*incultes*."

they divide interpretative problems into the discrete spheres of external uses and internal analyses. The formalistic attempt to constitute the text as an autotelic entity and to restrict history to background information is the *frère ennemi* of the historiographical attempt to construe texts as narrowly informational documents and to distance history from an internal, formalistic literary criticism. The two attempts arise together and covertly reinforce one another.

What then is an alternative that envisions both a different understanding of literary texts and a different relationship between historiography and literary criticism? Here one seeks a process of inquiry that, while not pretending to be a "totalizing" synthesis of analytically defined opposites, enables one to situate differently the valid aspects of more documentary and formalistic methods. A move in a desirable direction is, I think, made when texts are understood as variable uses of language that come to terms with— or "inscribe"—contexts in various ways—ways that engage the interpreter as historian *and* critic in an exchange with the past through a reading of texts.

Contexts of interpretation are at least three-fold; those of writing, reception, and critical reading.

Contexts of writing include the intentions of the author as well as more immediate biographical, sociocultural, and political situations with their ideologies and discourses. They also involve discursive institutions such as traditions and genres. I have already indicated that the novel, the proverbial "baggy monster," is a particularly open and contested genre in relation to which formalism was a prescriptive undertaking—a way of telling novelists to clean up their act. (The prescriptive incentive is quite evident in Percy Lubbock's *The Craft of Fiction*.) It is of course significant that formalism in both Russia and the West arose largely with poetry as its primary frame of reference, and poetry has been more subject to an "internal" history of conventions than has the novel. Even Harold Bloom, who applies psychoanalytic models to the history of poetry, presents this history largely as an *affaire entre poètes*. But, both in Bloom's work and more generally, the question is one of degree, for poetry has of course had exchanges with religious and other discourses, and the novel does relate to other novels. One consideration of general significance is that all contexts are encountered through the "medium" of specific texts or practices, and they must be reconstituted on the basis of textual evidence. For the past arrives in the form of texts and textualized remainders—memories, reports, published writings, archives, monuments, and so forth. The difficulties in the process of inferentially reconstructing contexts on the basis of texts (in the large sense) are often obscured or repressed, especially when one is convinced that a context or a set of contexts must be a determinative force with full explanatory power. The supplementary point is that texts interact with one another and with contexts in complex ways, and the specific question for interpretation is precisely how a text comes to terms with its putative contexts. This question is prematurely foreclosed when a text is understood in a narrowly documentary or a purely formalistic manner.

The novel has a distinguishing characteristic vis-à-vis historiography that is obvious but important. It may borrow from a documentary repertoire, and this process brings into play a carry-over effect that invalidates a conception of the novel in terms of pure fiction or a total suspension of reference to "external" reality. For example, the fact that Charles Bovary is an *officier de santé* is significant, and contextual knowledge concerning the nature and the relatively low social status of this occupation is necessary for certain aspects of the novel to be effective. When Emma's father represses the carnivalesque gesture of a fishmonger-relative, who squirts water through the keyhole of the bridal chamber, on the grounds that it is out of keeping with the dignity of his son-in-law, the father's act is situationally ironic and absurd, but the reader would not see it in this light without contextual knowledge. Decontextualization itself, which has been a forceful movement in modern literature, depends for its effect upon contextual expectations. But the novel, unlike historiography, may invent characters and events and give rise to configurations that are not available in the writing of history. When this elementary distinction between history and the novel breaks down, one has the appearance of myth. It is on other levels of interpretation, composition, and style that the relations between the novel and historiography become more engaging and controversial. In this regard, one might well compare the modulations of irony in Tocqueville, Stendhal, and Flaubert or argue that the reading of the times in *The Old Regime and the Revolution* is in certain ways comparable to that in *The Red and the Black* (for example, in its disclosure of the atomization of individuals and groups in society), while in other ways close to that in *Madame Bovary* (for example, in its own excavating use of irony).

Contexts of reception pose the problem of how texts are read, used, and abused in different social groups, institutions, and settings. These may be institutions or settings such as trials, schools, and studies as well as social formations such as disciplines, parties, movements, and political regimes. Professional readers, for example literary critics, are a significant group in the reception of literature, for they help to shape judgment and to teach others how to read (or, indeed, how to write). With reference to disciplines, book reviews are especially valuable indices of the operational structure of an organized branch of knowledge, and it is of course important to read reviews as reflections on their writers as well as on the objects of criticism.

In historiography, the kind of reader-response criticism (or aesthetics of reception) that is gaining currency is the most restricted empirical and analytic variant. The study of reception may even threaten to displace entirely the study of texts themselves, especially insofar as reception is a representative measure of collective "mentality" and amenable to conventional techniques of statistical and content analysis.[6] One may even behold the bizarre spectacle of "critics" who abandon criticism, confine themselves

6. See, for example, James Smith Allen, "History and the Novel: *Mentalité* in Modern Popular Fiction," *History and Theory* 22 (1983): 233–52. Allen applies to artifacts on the level of reception (for example, letters to the author) the same method of reading that Louis Chevalier applies to texts themselves.

to reporting how other readers read, and try to leave posterity with as little indication as possible of their own "response" as readers of texts. Here one must insist on the importance of critical reading itself as a context of reception—critical reading both of texts and of the ways they are read, used, and abused. Only through an attempted critical reading can one acquire some perspective on what occurs in the "reception" of texts in given contexts. And one simultaneously confronts the problem of the location of one's own reading in the contemporary critical scene.

The restriction of a study of reception to an empirical and analytic account of past readings or uses of texts is a neopositivistic attempt drastically to curtail one's own exchange with the past and, by the same token, to transcend the contemporary conflict of interpretations. It is also a blatant return to a narrowly documentary model of knowledge—one that threatens to identify all interpretation as anachronistic. One might even argue that it is a disavowal of the critical component of cognitively responsible research. Its recent counterpart on a more formalistic level is the exclusive "semiotic" or structural emphasis on the role of conventions, paradigms, or codes in prefiguring a range of readings. Indeed the convention or code may be seen on the model of a covering law that presents a use of language or a text as a straightforward instantiation or illustration of a discursive structure or an ideology. (For example, *Madame Bovary* may be construed as being essentially an illustration of the ideology of pure art which has escapist or defeatist political implications in the "real" world.)[7]

7. Thus Jerrold Seigel writes: "Even Flaubert's most frenzied and orgiastic visions were linked in his mind with (in Victor Brombert's words) 'an unmedicable [sic] sense of sadness and futility.' This is not the consciousness of an ideological revolutionary. . . . For Flaubert the carnivalesque served the project of pure art by demonstrating that no ideal could be realized in actual life. It was a constant reminder that art alone—even with all its participations in the disillusionments of life—remained the sole ground on which the ideal could be pursued. . . . The writer for whom the highest aspiration of art was *faire rêver* may make himself available for enlistment in whatever ideological projects we conceive, but thus to

All uses of language are of course coded to some extent. But the relation of any code or set of codes to actual usage may be intricate, and the nature of the interaction of a text with codes or ideological contexts is not a foregone conclusion. Highly stereotypical texts such as popular romances, commercials, and political propaganda tend to be highly coded and ideologically saturated because they are premised on the desire to get a delimited message through to the reader or listener. More complex texts such as significant novels have a more tangled relation to codes. A compelling consideration is that an ideology or code, especially when it engages deepseated desires or prejudices, exercises constraint over discourse, and no text, however exceptional, is entirely immune from this process or lucid about its operation. As Louis Althusser has argued, ideology "interpellates" or addresses the subject. Through politically interested "recognition scenes," it plays a role in constituting one's precritical sense of identity.

It should thus be obvious that a crucial issue in interpretation is that of the relation among symptomatic (or ideologically reinforcing), critical, and transformative tendencies in the way a text renders its pertinent codes and contexts. Some texts are themselves especially significant in the way they come to terms with this issue, and within limits they may serve as a "model" for the reader who is alert to certain considerations. No level of culture or genre has an absolute privilege in this respect, but the novel has been particularly rich in texts in which the relation to ideology is complicated by forcefully critical or even potentially transformative effects. Not

---

take him into our service is to project our features onto him, not to clarify his own." (*Journal of Modern History* 52 [1984]: 160.) Seigel not only envisions pure art as the essential meaning of the text; he dismisses more complex interpretations as projective and ideologically motivated. In this manner he identifies his own view with simple historical truth that merely clarifies Flaubert's own projects—as if the interpretation of Flaubert as an unqualified defeatist and escapist did not have ideological implications, especially for the academic liberal who has become disenchanted with earlier radical leanings. For a different view of Flaubert, see Dominick LaCapra, *"Madame Bovary" on Trial* (Ithaca, 1982). (The above-quoted passage is taken from Seigel's review of this book.)

only has it been a peculiarly restive genre that has assimilated other genres and tested the limits of its own generic definition. Its history has been punctuated by exceptional texts that seem to rewrite the genre and engage in many-voiced relations to earlier novels and to other signifying practices from the journalistic to the philosophical or religious. In fact the most telling question posed by the novel to historiography may be whether contemporary historical writing can learn something of a self-critical nature from a mode of discourse it has often tried to use or to explain in overly reductive fashion. A different way of reading novels may alert us not only to the contestatory voices and counter-discourses of the past but to the ways in which historiography itself may become a more critical voice in the "human sciences."

   In the absence of a concern with critical reading and a sensitivity to the problematic relation between texts and contexts, the great temptation of historiography is to veer in the direction of over-contextualization. Historians are completely at home with the idea that an account may fall short by not providing sufficient context, but we are likely to balk at the notion of over-contextualization or even to see it as nonsensical. How can one have too much context, especially if "reality" is identified with "context" and historical understanding is defined as a function of contextualization? Yet over-contextualization is not only possible; it is frequently a clear and present danger in the writing of history. It occurs when one so immerses a text in the particularities of its own time and place that one impedes responsive understanding and excessively restricts the interaction between past and present. Over-contextualization that effectively cuts history off from critical response linking past and present is an ideological service rendered to society by neo-positivistic and antiquarian approaches alike. It is at times the defect in the virtue of massive erudition when erudition replaces thought. There is no abstract criterion one can invoke to distinguish necessary from surplus contextualization, but the judgment and tact required to decide when the quest for context has gone too far are necessary complications in research, especially in intellectual history.

I would like to conclude by returning briefly to a broad issue that is much debated at present: the role of a canon in the selection of "significant" texts. Both feminist and Marxist criticism have brought out the intellectual and sociopolitical tendentiousness of the idea that there is a single canon of texts or artifacts, notably one made up of an exclusive list of high-cultural items such as "great" novels. The critique of a canon has an obvious and forceful bearing on intellectual history that I would not deny. But I would reject the quasi-ritualistic belief that a text is hopelessly contaminated by its function in a canon and that the alternative strategy should be to focus, more or less exclusively, on more "representative" artifacts, such as items of popular culture that have traditionally been omitted from the canon of elite monuments. I have tried to argue that this kind of professional populism often functions as a methodological way of making a scapegoat of high culture or its bearers, and, at least in historiography, it engenders the vicious paradox by which a certain class of scholars establish their own disciplinary hegemony through a vicarious appeal to the oppressed of the past.

I have also indicated that the larger setting in which the questions raised by a "canon" should be situated is that of the actual and desirable relations between popular and high culture—relations complicated by the impact of commodified culture. The effects of a commodity system upon culture are mystified as much by a fixation on a formalistic or purely hermeneutic appropriation of elite monuments as by a puristic missionary zeal or bright-eyed boosterism in advocating the study of popular culture. The obvious problem is how to relate a noncanonical or contestatory reading of high-cultural artifacts, such as "great" novels, and the investigation of artifacts, such as "popular" novels, that have traditionally been excluded from elite canons. My contention has been that students of culture, especially in the highly commodified modern period, have fewer chances of being critical and self-critical if they have not developed certain abilities in an exchange with cultural artifacts that themselves have particularly critical or even transformative relations to commodified culture. These artifacts may be found in both popular and high culture, and the crucial problem may not be whether a given artifact is part of an established canon (anticanonical approaches are in the process of creating their own canons) but whether it has been subjected to canonical interpretations and uses that are open to question. The point may not be simply to reject a *Bildungsideal;* it may be to give it a new shape by bringing it into contact with intellectual and sociopolitical issues from which it has often served as a refuge.

6

Conclusion

Historical method is no more than a recognized and tested
way of extracting from what the past has left the true
facts and events of that past, and so far as possible their
true meaning and interrelation, the whole governed by the
first principle of historical understanding, namely that the
past must be studied in its own right, for its own sake,
and on its own terms. . . . None of this may sound very
satisfactory, and there need be no doubt that the quality
of the historian will always determine the quality of his
research. Nevertheless, the procedure outlined reduces this
personal element and offers valuable safeguards because it
depends on two things: a real training in the craft
practised, and a real concern with history (the past as
such) rather than with the formulation of theories about it.

G. R. ELTON, *The Practice of History*

THIS book is obviously polemical in its attempt to rethink
certain assumptions and procedures of the historical craft. It
is intended as a critical intervention in a profession where debates
about self-understanding and practice are not as prevalent as I
think they should be. As a polemic, this book contains a measure of
exaggeration and a stylization of arguments. In spite of the difficulty of ever providing convincing proofs of large-scale judgments,
I would contend that I do not simply set up "straw men." I think

the exaggerations bring into relief prevalent features of current historiography that are indeed open to question.

My polemic has as one of its reference points the issue of the relation between history and criticism, including the role of self-reflection that is not autonomized but instead pointedly related to historiographical practice. For many historians at present, history and criticism are two incompatible genres. History is like an owl that in its age-old wisdom knows it must stay close to the ground. Critical theory is like an eagle that soars skyward in quest of its prey. When the eagle tries to mate with the owl, the result is one loud screech.

My love of allegory cannot bring me to endorse this Aesopian fable. Not only can history and criticism coexist. Their union may engender vital and hardy stock. Indeed, in its absence, each becomes weaker through excessive inbreeding. Yet the biological analogy is of course itself faulty. Another analogy is perhaps better. It is as acceptable to join history and criticism as it is to have description, dramatic dialogue, and reflective soliloquy in the same novel. (Witness *The Brothers Karamazov* and *Doctor Faustus*.)

In more general terms, my polemic has a point to the extent that a book such as G. R. Elton's *The Practice of History* (1967) represents conventional wisdom in the historical profession. In significant ways Elton does crystallize views prevalent among historians. Indeed so much is this the case that I would readily agree with many of his specific pointers or rules-of-thumb for teaching and research. But I would see them as components of a largely "documentary" model of knowledge that is necessary but not sufficient for historical research, particularly in a field such as intellectual history.

What would I disagree with in Elton's account? One thing would be the rhetoric of "the truth," especially in the overly authoritative strains in which Elton intones it. This rhetoric is not required as a rationale for his sober, salutary, and witty reformulation of what may often deserve to be conventional wisdom in the craft. It does, however, function as a common-sense metaphysical foundation for Elton's belief that all historians should be doing basically the same thing: general narrative synthesis, unobtrusively punctuated by analytic interludes and held together by a determined focus on a dominant theme (for Elton, politics). "The truth" amounts to "objective" documentary reconstruction presented in classically ordered form; it requires the ostracism or castigation of those historians who do not subscribe to the one true way of practicing history.

I would also question the idea that if one does not accept Elton's rhetoric, one is forced to line up with E. H. Carr and the "relativists." A standard practice in historiography seminars is to begin by assigning Elton's *The Practice of History* and Carr's *What Is History?* (1962) as representing the alternatives in the self-understanding of the discipline. This practice is sure to generate heated debate among students, and it starts a course with a pleasant "Steve Reeves meets Godzilla" scenario. The result is usually a more or less pragmatic and eclectic "synthesis" of the two works that may serve as a tenuous consensus on which the seminar may proceed in its study of less "theoretical" or "methodological" assignments.

The argument in the present book is that extreme documentary objectivism and relativistic subjectivism do not constitute genuine alternatives. They are mutually supportive parts of the same larger complex. The objectivist historian places the past in the "logocentric" position of what Jacques Derrida calls the "transcendental signified." It is simply there in its sheer reality, and the task of the historian is to use sources as documents to reconstruct past reality as objectively as he or she can. The objectivist falsely sees the attempt to question precritical and unreflective certainty about the nature of history as tantamount to denying that people really bleed when they are cut—and that they do not bleed signification. The relativist simply turns objectivist "logocentrism" upside-down. The historian places himself or herself in the position of

"transcendental signifier" that "produces" or "makes" the meaning of the past. And in the semiotic variant of relativism, the past
does indeed seem submerged in all-pervasive semiosis.

The most striking characteristic of a book such as Elton's—one
it by and large shares with Carr's—is not what it explicitly argues
but what it tacitly assumes (or even excludes). Elton not only
assumes that objectivism and relativism exhaust the field of possibilities in historical self-understanding. He reverts to the most
classical conception of a book as a unified whole, and he exhorts
the historian to resort to any device, however superficial, to under-
line coherence and continuity both in his or her account and in the
historical process. He attempts to rehabilitate narrative as at least
the equal of analysis in historiography, but his conception of
narrative is extremely conventional. In fact he tacitly positions
both narrative and analysis within a model of historical knowledge
whereby texts and documents are reduced to quarries for facts
about some other privileged "reality." Elton also omits any mention of literature and philosophy, even in a narrowly documentary
conception of them. They apparently have no role to play in the
practice of history either as "evidence" or as areas that may foster
cricial self-reflection among historians themselves. Nor is there any
discussion of intellectual history as a valid subdiscipline of historical research (although there is much shadow boxing with social
history). Elton's model of documentary knowledge construes
sources solely as evidence in the reconstruction of phenomena
external to them, and it is simply too restricted for research in
intellectual history. Its application lends itself to an excessive focus
on topics whose very terms are set by other subdisciplines (for
example, political or social history), and it often induces dubious
protocols of research (for example, the idea that everything hap-
pening in a text is simply evidence in the reconstruction of an
intention or a *mentalité*). Certain procedures Elton enumerates are
of course relevant to all historical research, and there must be
interaction among subdisciplines on important topics common to
the profession as a whole. But, taken *tout court*, the model Elton

relies on would result at best in an overly corseted and confined practice that eliminates too many aspects of a cognitively responsible but still responsive exchange between past and present.

This book may thus be seen as a contestatory supplement to the views of a historian such as Elton. It is because of dissatisfaction with established procedures, procedures tying history too closely to narrowly documentary reconstruction of a precritically conceived past, that some historians have recently turned to other disciplines and newer interpretative approaches. At present critics must attempt to be both more discriminating and more specific in articulating what they question in conventional historiography and what they propose for historical self-understanding and practice.

I have suggested that the notion (or the root metaphor) of dialogic interchange with the past has value in the attempt to rethink historiography in significantly different terms. I have tried to elucidate some of its implications and its bearing on the necessary "documentary" components of historiography. I have also brought it into contact with the difficult idea of "transference," which I think requires further reflection if one is to arrive at a better understanding of historical inquiry. Following the lead of such theorists as Clifford Geertz and T. S. Kuhn, recent historians sensitive to problems of reading and interpretation have put forth the view that inquiry into the past should begin at points where a document seems most opaque and alien. This often fruitful methodological dictum may, however, become misleading when it leads to a resuscitation of the simplistic belief in the all but total difference between the past and the present. It is true that some periods may be initially as strange as exotic societies studied by anthropologists, and this strangeness often becomes accentuated the further back one travels in time. But the unproblematic assertion of the radical alterity of the past is often the complement of an excessively homogeneous conception of the present (or the self), and it readily induces a lack of critical self-reflection and a denial or repression of transferential relations toward the "other." For most readers today, the texts of Derrida or Heidegger may well appear more alien than the views of a bourgeois or even a peasant or an artisan during the Old Regime. Alterity, in other words, is not simply "out there" in the past but in "us" as well, and the comprehensive problem in inquiry is how to understand and to negotiate varying degrees of proximity and distance in the relation to the "other" that is both outside and inside ourselves. Dwelling on the wonderful strangeness of the past may turn into a pretext for avoiding what unsettles one's own protocols of inquiry and troubles the flow of a narrative.

One of the largest issues broached in this book is that of the relation among texts, discursive practices, and sociopolitical institutions. I have argued that this issue is resolved in oversimplified fashion both by an internal history of ideas and by a sociology of knowledge (or a social history of ideas). The challenge posed to history is how to address this issue in a manner that sets up a mutually informative and provocative interaction between both subdisciplines in historiography and the disciplines in general. There is an important sense in which inquiry into the relation between texts and institutions constitutes a project that links all the humanities and social sciences. Discursive practices such as genres and intellectual disciplines create constraints and possibilities for specific uses of language such as texts. And discursive practices always have a significant relation to sociopolitical institutions—a relation that becomes obvious and subject to sanctions once intellectual pursuits are formally organized in institutionalized disciplines. Conventional or stereotypical texts conform most to set discursive and institutional expectations, while the exceptional text has a more problematic relation both to discursive practices it is placing in question and to those it is helping to engender. Indeed one key function of epigones would seem to be to reduce the problematic texts of "initiators of discursive practices" (in Foucault's phrase) to their generic or paradigmatic level, thereby making them more adaptable to certain institutional uses. The more challenging and, at times, disconcerting text seems to rewrite the genre or to take part in a continual founding and altering of expectations. The apparent paradox is that texts hailed as perfections of a genre or a discursive practice may also test and contest its limits. One question to be addressed by an investigation of texts and discursive practices is how texts classified as "great" or as "classics" are construed in canonical interpretations and whether it may be argued that those texts engage processes that are repressed or downplayed in canonical interpretations—processes that may in certain situations have broader social and political consequences. The more general problem is the way all documents are texts that rework what they "represent" and thus make a difference in the sociopolitical and discursive context in which they are inserted. The transferential dimension of research makes this a problem not only in the phenomena of the past that we study but in the very way in which we study them—the language we use and abuse in coming to terms with them.

Stated in the simplest possible manner, the question active in this book concerns the kind of relation one should have to the past in professional historiography and beyond it. A "documentary" model serves the craft well on a purely professional level, but it does not do enough either for historians or for other groups in society. The danger in more experimental approaches is the seeming inability to address significant dimensions of the past and the tendency to reprocess its "traces" in involuted terms that often appear projective and self-involved. An even greater danger is a lemming-like fascination for discursive impasses and an obsessive interest in the aberrant and aleatory—tendencies that threaten to identify all controlling limits with totalizing mastery and thus to undermine any conception of critical rationality. The virtue of traditional historiography at its best has been an ability to join meticulous research with a form of critical rationality in the investigation of the past. I in no sense want to abandon that virtue. Instead I would like to see it emerge fortified through a confrontation with contemporary challenges that may be interpreted to indicate the need—both in the historical profession and beyond it—for a conception of reason open to certain contestatory "voices." These voices are not mere hermeneutic echoes that reso- nate on the level of pure meaning; they have implications for the conduct of social and political life, including life within academic disciplines. One thing an institution should be is a setting for a dialogic encounter in which limiting norms necessary for life in common are put to tests that may strengthen or transform them. Indeed a humanistic discipline remains vital to the extent it is possible within it to engage points of view that pose fundamental questions to one's own. The difficulty is to create the material and intellectual conditions in which such an exchange is actually possible.

Index

Library of Congress Cataloging in Publication Data

LaCapra, Dominick, 1939–
  History and criticism.

  Includes index.
  1. Historiography. I. Title.
D13.L26 1985   907'.2   84-16990
ISBN 0-8014-1788-0 (alk. paper)
ISBN 0-8014-9324-2 (pbk.: alk. paper)